Surgical Philosophy

Concepts of Modern Surgery Paralleled to Sun Tzu's 'Art of War'

Surgical Philosophy

Concepts of Modern Surgery Paralleled to Sun Tzu's 'Art of War'

Hutan Ashrafian

Clinical Lecturer in Surgery
Faculty of Medicine
Imperial College London, UK

CRC Press
Taylor & Francis Group
Boca Raton London New York

CRC Press is an imprint of the
Taylor & Francis Group, an **informa** business

CRC Press
Taylor & Francis Group
6000 Broken Sound Parkway NW, Suite 300
Boca Raton, FL 33487-2742

© 2016 by Taylor & Francis Group, LLC
CRC Press is an imprint of Taylor & Francis Group, an Informa business

No claim to original U.S. Government works

Printed on acid-free paper
Version Date: 20150629

International Standard Book Number-13: 978-1-4987-3277-2 (Paperback)

Visit the Taylor & Francis Web site at
http://www.taylorandfrancis.com

and the CRC Press Web site at
http://www.crcpress.com

Contents

Preface

The treatment of disease consists of a combative struggle between a curative therapy and a pathological affliction. As such, the action of achieving a cure can be likened to successfully waging war on sickness and bodily disorders. This metaphor of medicine and war is most germane when considered in the context of surgery, where a surgeon literally manipulates body tissues to achieve successful healing or to effectively manage illness. This requires the application of surgical tools or weapons-like 'armaments' to create incisions, cuts and reconstructions for removing the disease source or enhancing the body's functions. Indeed in popular culture, many war-like activities are described from a surgical perspective; for example the term 'surgical strike' (or 'strike with surgical precision') represents a military operation such as an air strike that results in minimal or no collateral damage to the nearby vicinity or populace. Alternatively, individuals in military special forces regularly consider their line of work to be akin to the role of an oncological surgeon, where they 'go in, remove a cancer and get out' – a metaphor that represents a military raid, the expedited slaying of an opponent and a timely escape. Typically this is reinforced with the adage that the mission was performed with 'clinical' precision.

Among the greatest treatises on combat strategy is the seminal text *The Art of War*, ascribed to the famed Chinese military scholar Sun Tzu (also known as Sunzi, Sun Zi and Sun Wu). This text is considered by many as the greatest manuscript in the canon of the Seven Military Classics of ancient China, and has been utilized by Eastern and Western warrior classes for centuries, ranging from Japanese Samurai, generals in modern warfare and even the legendary ninja. More recently in the twentieth century this text was more widely disseminated for broader use in business strategy, leadership studies and management consultancy as a text for application in the modern business world.

Although *The Art of War* is considered by popular belief to be authored by Sun Tzu (primarily by ancient Chinese sources), this claim is shrouded with controversy. Some of the few direct facts we have regarding this text include the unearthing of a nearly complete version of the book from a tomb at Yinqueshan Hill, Linyi City, Shandong Province, China, in June 1974. The chance archaeological discovery was made due to building excavations for a health ministry building, where bamboo strips were found and washed to uncover writing as part of a bamboo book originating from the Han Dynasty. The text was readily recognized as *The Art of War*, which consequently dates the book to at least the Han period (206 BCE–220 CE), which was the second imperial dynasty of China.

Most traditionalists, however, attribute the book to the sixth-century BCE, as a historical figure listed to be Sun Tzu was recorded as having existed during this time in two classic Chinese texts, *The Records of the Grand Historian* (also known as the *Shiji*) written by Sima Qian between 109 BC and 91 BC, and *The Spring and Autumn Annals* (during the period 722 BCE–481 BCE) purported by the philosopher Mencius to have been written by Confucius (of whom he was the greatest supporter), though now generally accepted to have been compiled by several scholars from the State of Lu. Although the historical character of Sun Tzu was mentioned, his association with the main text is still uncertain. According to modern legends, however, he was considered the greatest military strategist of the ancient world, whose genius was saved in the form of *The Art of War.*

Although there is a known commonality in military language used between *The Art of War* and the other Seven Military Classics of ancient China that may imply an influence of these from *The Art of War* on the other books of the canon, there is an equal and opposing possibility that the other books of the canon influenced *The Art of War*, thereby further complicating its origins.

The author of the book, whether Sun Tzu or another individual or individuals, was unlikely to have generated all the concepts of warfare innately, and there is a possibility that the book was derived from ancient teachings or even earlier books. The book is popularly believed to derive from the mid-to-late Warring States period (or Era of Warring States/Warring Kingdoms) between circa 403 and 475 BCE and 221 BCE, a time when there were numerous internal conflicts in ancient China between territories and warlords competing over the areas of (i) Qin in the West, (ii) Chu in the South, (iii) Qi in Shandong, (iv) Yan near Beijing in the North, and the centrally placed (v) Han, (vi) Wei and (vii) Zhao. It was only during this time that several of the book's events and examples could have taken place.

As a result, even if Sun Tzu were the author of the book, it would have been modified after his death to account for such events, or alternatively may not have been written by him at all.

The oldest existing fragments of *The Art of War*, or texts on which it is derived, are dated to the later fifth-century BC, predating the likely lifetime of Sun Tzu, whereas some of the virtues listed for commanders closely follow the philosophy of Confucianism that may have coincided with the time of the historical Sun Tzu during the Spring and Autumn Period (771 to 476–403 BCE) or after his death in the Han period (206 BCE to 220 CE).

We are therefore uncertain as to the time that *The Art of War* was written, although this would have occurred during or before the Han Dynasty (206 BCE–220 CE), and we are also uncertain as to whether a historical character named Sun Tzu was its author. Nevertheless, ever since its modern translation into French by the Jesuit missionary Jean Joseph in 1772 the Western world increasingly appreciated this work as a seminal treatise applicable to warfare and daily existence, while it has had a consistent and continual appreciation in the Orient. The questions of whether or not the historical Sun Tzu wrote the book and whether or not he was the military genius who is recounted in modern legends have now been surpassed by the concept that Sun Tzu's *The Art of War* is more of a recognizable title for the book than an accurate statement of its origins. It stands as one of the greatest military masterpieces of all time, originating from approximately 2000 years ago with likely early proto-versions deriving from even earlier manuscripts of warfare.

The original book consists of thirteen sections that have been listed to equip potential commanders for all aspects of warfare. As I have earlier identified the similarities between waging wars and combating disease through surgery, I have therefore written this surgically orientated text along the guidelines listed in Sun Tzu's *The Art of War*. My choice of translation was the 1910 version of Lionel Giles CBE (1875–1958, son of H.A. Giles, Professor of Chinese at Cambridge), whose work is the most familiar and popularized adaption in the English-speaking world. Although there has been some controversy as to the precision of this 100-year-old translation, which necessarily exists with all such works, its concepts are broadly accepted.

The current book therefore employs the analogy of waging warfare to that of fighting disease. Rather than using Sun Tzu's book literally as waging war on other individuals or states, its use is to apply the same principles and concepts to 'wage war' on pathology through surgery. This is in essence the role of the surgeon and can offer new insights into treating patients. The mounting parallels between political strategy and those of molecular biology are increasingly understood through biopolitics. Typically this considers the application of biological principles and analogies for appraising political, cultural and philosophical activity. However, the reverse is also valid where political actions can offer analogies to biological effects (see Ashrafian H., *Science.* 2009 Jan 30;323[5914]:582. Systems politics and political systems); this is the core principle of this manuscript.

This metaphor has been used in other contexts; for example in his well-known pre–World War II Quarantine Speech (1937), President Franklin Delano Roosevelt pronounced that 'war is a contagion'. Comparable analogies include those of a national revolution or civil war akin to autoimmunity, where the body's immune system essentially attacks itself. Alternatively, some sociopolitical and policy interventions can be considered as protective 'vaccines' from future socioeconomic problems.

The text in this book reflects the strategies and philosophies of arguably the most famed book of army battles in the context of waging war on disease through the use of surgery. The role of the surgeon in this text is equivalent to that of a leader or military commander and the lessons offered in Sun Tzu's *The Art of War* are expanded to identify surgical principles and practice.

The following eleven sections of Sun Tzu's books are therefore transformed into a surgical paradigm in the following manner:

1. *Laying Plans* – The Aims of Operative Surgery
2. *Waging War* – Performing Surgery
3. *Attack by Stratagem* – Surgical Strategies
4. *Tactical Dispositions* – Surgical Decision Making
5. *Energy* – Operative Methodology
6. *Maneuvering* – Civilization
7. *Variation in Tactics* – Approaches and Leadership
8. *Terrain* – Anatomy
9. *The Nine Situations* – The Nine Elements of the Surgical Sieve and Surgical Specialties
10. *The Attack by Fire* – Firesticks and Haemostasis
11. *The Use of Spies* – Imaging

Each section goes on to reflect the messages in *The Art of War* with a modern surgical healthcare point of view. The goal for any doctor or surgeon is to improve the care and medical outcomes of his or her patients. The inspiration of this book is a direct extension of that mindset where patient safety, best evidence, personalized healthcare and precision medicine are the true goals of treatment strategies and surgery.

As Sun Tzu's *The Art of War* is considered a book for military strategy and tactics for commanders in the armed forces, the goal of this book is to offer principles, strategies and leadership guidelines for surgeons and all healthcare practitioners who carry out interventional procedures for the ultimate aim of defeating illness and enhancing the care of their patients.

The Author

Hutan Ashrafian is a clinical lecturer in surgery based at Imperial College London. His work focuses on the surgical resolution of metabolic syndrome- and obesity-related diseases ranging from cardiac dysfunction to diabetes and cancer. He has authored over 250 peer-reviewed publications and has been awarded research fellowships from the Wellcome Trust, National Institute for Health Research, the Hunterian Prize and the Arris and Gale Lectureship of The Royal College of Surgeons of England. His PhD on the global metabolic signature of bariatric surgery received several prizes including an Academy of Medical Sciences award. His research interests include the development of state-of-the-art approaches for bio-inspired regenerative technologies, the application of artificial intelligence and robotics to modern surgical practice, the enhancement of evidence synthesis in healthcare and the development of novel models of innovation and economics in health policy.

Cover Illustration

The famous Chinese surgeon Hua Tuo (Ka Da c. 140–208 CE) operates on the wounded arm of General Guan Yu (Kan U c. 150–219). The image represents a story in the historical fourteenth-century novel *Romance of the Three Kingdoms* by Luo Guanzhong.

In the story, Guan Yu injured his right arm after being struck with a poisoned arrow during the Battle of Fancheng in 219. Hua Tuo suggested that treatment would require surgical exploration and excision of foreign tissue from the wound, and offered that Guan Yu should have the procedure performed under anaesthesia. At this Guan Yu laughed, informing the surgeon that he was not afraid of pain, and subsequently demonstrated this by stoically playing a game of GO (wéiqí) with his fellow officer Ma Liang

(Jichang c. 187–222) while the surgeon operated on his arm (despite the gratuitous surgical sounds and sights of the procedure). The story recounts the procedure as 'scraping the poison from the bone'. The operation was successful and Hua Tuo was offered a large reward in the form of 100 ounces of gold and a sumptuous banquet, which he modestly declined. Notably, the historical Battle of Fancheng in 219 is considered to have taken place 11 years after the estimates of Hua Tuo's lifetime.

The woodblock triptych print from Utagawa Kuniyoshi (歌川国芳) (1797–1861) in 1853 (Edo period) demonstrates surgical equipment and the application of a haemorrhage-protecting tourniquet to the right arm while the operation is being performed. (Image used with permission from the British Museum Company Limited, London, UK.)

1 The Aims of Operative Surgery

1. Sun Tzu said: The art of war is of vital importance to the State.

1. The art of surgery is of vital importance to modern medicine and is a key component of modern healthcare.

2. It is a matter of life and death, a road either to safety or to ruin. Hence it is a subject of inquiry which can on no account be neglected.

2. It is a matter of life and death; a path to successful outcomes and patient satisfaction or medical complications, poor outcomes and death. As a result it should be studied and on no account can it be neglected by doctors and health practitioners.

3. The art of war, then, is governed by five constant factors, to be taken into account in one's deliberations, when seeking to determine the conditions obtaining in the field.

3. The art of surgery is governed by five constant factors; these require consideration in one's thoughts, analyses and decision making when reflecting on a surgical problem or assessing a patient.

4. These are: (1) The Moral Law; (2) Heaven; (3) Earth; (4) The Commander; (5) Method and discipline.

4. These are (1) Patient Safety and Ethics; (2) Science, Anatomy and Research; (3) Operating Environment and Staff; (4) The Surgeon; and (5) Surgical Training (Figure 1.1).

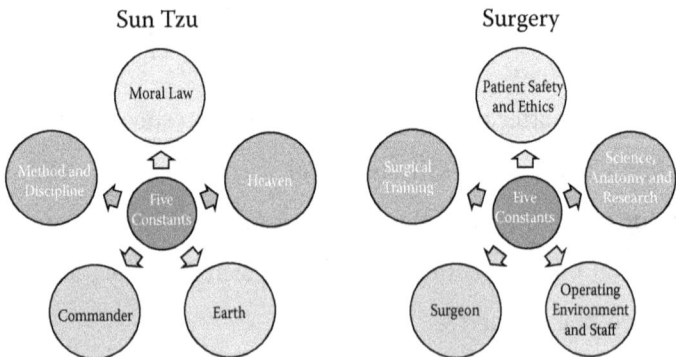

Figure 1.1 The five constant factors.

5, 6. The Moral Law causes the people to be in complete accord with their ruler, so that they will follow him regardless of their lives, undismayed by any danger.

5, 6. Patient Safety and Ethics allows doctors and health practitioners to be in complete accord with their fundamental values, so that they will follow these regardless of their careers, undismayed by complex pathologies and dangerous diseases.

7. Heaven signifies night and day, cold and heat, times and seasons.

7. Science, Anatomy and Research represents the knowledge of the human body, its diseases and treatments. Surgery cannot take place without a deep-rooted understanding of anatomy and surgical practice cannot occur without scientific principles and methods. The advancement of surgery can only take place through the objectivity and lack of bias offered by the scientific method in the practice of surgical research. This includes characterizations (definitions, observations, measurements), hypothesis development, predictions from the hypotheses (logical deduction and reasoning), experiments (testing), evaluation and improvement and confirmation. These processes have come to us from luminaries including Aristotle

(384–322 BCE), Alhazen (c. 965–1040), Francis Bacon (1561–1626), Galileo Galilei (1564–1642) and Karl Popper (1902–1994, father of critical rationalism) but have been increasingly adopted by surgeons in the nineteenth, twentieth and twenty-first centuries.

All surgical practice should be based on the best evidence so that all surgeons should adhere to evidence-based surgery. Research data is required to support surgical decisions and actions, and the raw knowledge of research (molecular data, individual case data, clinical trial data, epidemiological data and policy data) is delivered into surgical practice through evidence synthesis. This offers the ability to combine all raw data from experiments whether quantitative or qualitative. Evidence synthesis techniques include a vast array of models and mathematical tools (including statistical tests and meta-analyses) to offer answers for surgical questions posed by individual surgeons, healthcare institutions, policymakers and even members of the public. This allows the practice of personalized evidence-based surgery and precision medicine. In patient care both research and audit are important elements of clinical governance and they have specific meanings. Research is related to the generation of new knowledge whereas audit is focussed on identifying how to improve certain practices and outcomes.

There is clearly an overlap although the two concepts are distinct and are readily applied in patient care. Surgery cannot proceed without the application of the scientific method as this allows the appropriate translation of new knowledge. Whether it reflects the design of a new surgical robot, novel surgical molecular therapy or even psychological support of surgical patients, the application of science offers new knowledge to enhance patients' treatments in a way that decreases inherent researcher biases but provides an environment of healthy generation of new surgical concepts.

8. Earth comprises distances, great and small; danger and security; open ground and narrow passes; the chances of life and death.

8. Operating environment and staff comprises the whole context in which operations take place. This includes the precision of operating instruments (from scalpel and diathermy to surgical robot). What is the patient pathway leading to the patient coming for an operation? What is the design and condition of the operating space or theatre? Is there for example conventional (mixing), plenum, laminar airflow (LAF or vertical parallel flow), directed airflow or combined ventilation? Who are the other theatre staff (assistant surgeon, anaesthetists, operating room practitioners)?

What is their expertise and experience? What are their work and nonwork relationships with each other, the room, the patient and the surgeon? All these factors relate to the technical and nontechnical skills of all theatre members and if all these interactions are enhanced then patient safety and patient outcomes can be optimized.

9. The Commander stands for the virtues of wisdom, sincerity, benevolence, courage and strictness.

9. The surgeon stands for the virtues of leadership, wisdom, sincerity, benevolence, courage and strictness. The role of the surgeon is to completely know the patient, understand the disease process and guide the patient through the patient pathway. This includes actually operating on the patient, but also encompasses the broader role of supporting disease diagnosis and management while also guiding or contributing to nonoperative patient care where necessary. The surgeon is regularly considered to be a leader in the patient pathway, and consequently the role of the surgeon is fundamentally central in decision making, team management, pathway regulation, communication and the development of patient management policies.

10. By method and discipline are to be understood the marshaling of the army in its proper subdivisions, the graduations of rank among the officers, the maintenance of roads by which supplies may reach the army, and the control of military expenditure.

10. The art of surgery cannot exit or grow without surgical training. Surgeons need to be trained not only to operate but to perform all the technical and nontechnical elements of surgery. The application of simulators and surgical learning curves has relevance in direct surgical training but these concepts carry a wider resonance in terms of patient management experience, team iteration and the role of the surgeon in wider society. The provenance of simulation in surgical training is typically considered to be a modern phenomenon largely as an offshoot of simulation first developed in nonmedical fields (such as the airline industry and simulators for pilots). In reality, however, surgical simulation dates back to before the eighth century BCE. In the ancient Zoroastrian text of the Vendidad translated by James Darmesteter (*Sacred Books of the East*, Volume 4, 1880, Oxford University Press) the following text from Chapter 7, Verses 36 to 40 relates to surgeons (Kard-pezeshks or knife-doctors) operating on True-Worshipers and Demon-Worshipers:

> [36.] O Maker of the material world, thou Holy One! If a *True-Worshiper* wants to practice the art of healing, on whom shall he first prove his skill? On *True-Worshiper*

or *Demon-Worshipers*? [37.] *The Lord* answered: '*Demon-Worshipers* shall he first prove himself, rather than on *True-Worshipers*. If he treat with the knife a *Demon-Worshiper* and he die; if he treat with the knife a second *Demon-Worshiper* and he die; if he treat with the knife for the third time a *Demon-Worshiper* and he die, he is unfit for ever and ever. [38.] 'Let him therefore never attend any *True-Worshiper*; let him never treat with the knife a *True-Worshiper*, nor wound him with the knife. If he shall ever attend any *True-Worshiper*, if he shall ever treat with the knife any *True-Worshiper*, and wound him with the knife, he shall pay for his wound the penalty for wilful murder. [39.] 'If he treat with the knife a *Demon-Worshiper* and he recover; if he treat with the knife a second *Demon-Worshiper* and he recover; if for the third time he treat with the knife a *Demon-Worshiper* and he recover; then he is fit for ever and ever. [40.] 'He may henceforth at his will attend *True-Worshipers*; he may at his will treat with the knife *True-Worshipers*, and heal them with the knife.'

This segment alludes that 'simulation' by surgery on three 'non-believers' with success would then allow a surgeon the right to operate on 'believers'. Modern simulation techniques apply computer-based technologies, artificial tissue and models and virtual worlds. Each surgical situation (whether technical or nontechnical) can ultimately be replicated by a simulated scenario, to offer an appropriate surgical training environment. Enhanced surgical training can offer higher quality surgeons, improved patient outcomes and ultimately enriched patient well-being.

11. These five heads should be familiar to every general: he who knows them will be victorious; he who knows them not will fail.

11. These five factors should be familiar to every surgeon: he or she who knows them will succeed in treating his or her patients; he or she who knows them not will fail.

12. Therefore, in your deliberations, when seeking to determine the military conditions, let them be made the basis of a comparison, in this wise:

12. Therefore, in your deliberations, when seeking to determine and treat the surgical conditions of your patient(s), let them be made the basis of the following comparison:

13. (1) Which of the two sovereigns is imbued with the Moral law? (2) Which of the two generals has most ability? (3) With whom lie the advantages derived from Heaven and Earth? (4) On which side is discipline most rigorously enforced? (5) Which army is stronger? (6) On which side are officers and men more highly trained? (7) In which army is there the greater constancy both in reward and punishment?

13. (1) Which of the two hospitals (or healthcare institutions) offer the most rigorous patient safety and ethics?

(2) Which of the two surgeons has the most ability?

(3) With whom lie the advantages derived from Science, Anatomy and Research, and which healthcare institute offers the best operating environment and staff, who offers the best value and quality of care with the most safety?

(4) On which side is adherence to national/international guidelines most rigorously enforced?

(5) Which healthcare institute offers the strongest professional staff, surgeons and researchers?

(6) On which side are the surgeons and surgical trainees more highly trained?

(7) In which healthcare institution is there the greater constancy in reward, incentivisation and support (or training) for failing staff?

14. By means of these seven considerations I can forecast victory or defeat.

14. By means of these seven considerations I can forecast surgical treatment success or failure.

15. The general that hearkens to my counsel and acts upon it, will conquer: let such a one be retained in command! The general that hearkens not to my counsel nor acts upon it, will suffer defeat: let such a one be dismissed!

15. The surgeon who reflects on this advice and acts upon it will conquer disease: Individuals such as these should be kept and promoted as surgeons! Surgeons who do not consider these elements and who do not act upon them will fare poorly in the face of disease – such individuals should not receive support in a career in surgery.

16. While heading the profit of my counsel, avail yourself also of any helpful circumstances over and beyond the ordinary rules.

16. While contemplating the benefits of my advice, expose yourself also to other useful sources of healthcare environments, centres and knowledge over and above the ordinary lessons.

17. According as circumstances are favorable, one should modify one's plans.

17. In surgery one needs to be both pragmatic and flexible. When operative circumstances are favourable, one should modify one's decisions and actions to offer the patient the best gains and outcomes.

18. All warfare is based on deception.

18. All surgery can benefit from biological deception. Many disease processes contain elements of molecular deception or

molecular mimicry where pathogens and disease processes utilize common molecular structures (genes-DNA, RNA or proteins) with healthy tissues to evade natural biological defences. For example cancer typically hijacks inherent biological structures and systems to generate cancer products, activating the phosphatidylinositide-3-OH kinase/3-phospho-inositide-dependent protein kinase-1 (PDK1)/Akt and the Raf/mitogen-activated protein kinase (MAPK/ERK) kinase (MEK)/mitogen-activated protein kinase (MAPK) pathways. Alternatively, pathogens utilize immune marker epitopes resembling natural human epitopes such as human leukocyte antigens (HLAs) of the major histocompatibility (MHC) molecule system to go 'under the immune radar'. As a result auto-immunity can result where the body unwittingly attacks itself in order to exterminate pathogens carrying these immune recognition molecules. Retroviruses such as the human immunodeficiency virus (HIV) hijack and therefore 'deceive' host cells to utilize the cells' own reverse transcriptase enzymes to produce DNA from its RNA genome to replicate and multiply this pathogenic lentivirus.

Surgeons, however, can also apply bio-deception tools in many guises to treat their patients.

The most common form of biological deception in surgery includes antibiotics such as those of the large β-lactam antibiotic family. Examples include the famous penicillin derivatives, cephalosporins, monobactams and carbapenems. These antibiotics all contain β-lactam segments, which are structural analogues to the D-alanyl-D-ala amino acid residues of the precursor NAM/NAG-peptide subunits of the peptidoglycan layer of the bacterial cell wall. When they are exposed to bacteria, antibiotics irreversibly bind to penicillin-binding proteins (PBPs) in competition with the reversible D-alanyl-D-alanine residues. As the PBPs regulate the final transpeptidation step in the synthesis of the peptidoglycan layer of the bacterial cell wall, further transpeptidation is limited and bacterial cell wall synthesis is disrupted and exposed. Consequently bacterial structural integrity and subsequent division is halted so that the bacteria cannot survive. As a result, β-lactam antibiotics are considered bactericidal and have saved millions of patient lives through bio-deception.

All forms of reconstructive techniques rely on deceiving the body's healing process to heal a surgical man-made construct. Whether two segments of bowel are anastomosed with sutures or anastomotic gun after the surgical resection of cancer or a coronary artery is bypassed with a surgical conduit (typically vein or artery), the surgeon is deceiving the natural inherent healing process to heal and functionally link two biological segments in the body. These healing processes were initially designed to support the body from the damage and trauma of living, however the surgeon utilizes these mechanisms to create human-selected biological outcomes. In some cases the surgical manipulation of the human body using its own healing processes can lead to more than just healing, and can result in super-human supra-physiological effects. Such manipulations can be defined as autobionics, a process of biological enhancement due to rearrangement of the body tissues in a formation for which the body had not initially been designed but rather was deceived into making. Examples include the Roux-en-Y gastric bypass procedure, which can lead to regeneration of the pancreas (neo-genesis) in some animal models, or achievement of pancreatic β-cell hyperplasia in humans to offer enhanced insulin release, resolution of type II diabetes mellitus and can even go beyond this to result in hypoglycaemic episodes. This autobionic effect can occur through the BRAVE (bile flow alteration, reduction of gastric size, anatomical gut rearrangement and altered flow of nutrients, vagal manipulation and subsequent enteric gut hormone modulation) effects. Here, for example, endocrine gut hormonal signals from rearranged gut and neuronal signals from manipulated or transected vagal nerves can deceive the body into enhancing its function in particular ways. Other auto-bionic examples include the biological 'deception' of the heart by replacing the tri-leaflet (semi-lunar from the high pressure chambers of the heart) aortic valve with the tri-leaflet tricuspid valve (semi-lunar valve from the low pressure chambers of the heart) in the pulmonary autograft Ross procedure to offer a higher valve tensile strength at the aortic site.

Surgical biological deception tools also include adjuvant and neo-adjuvant biological mimics in the form of anti-cancer vaccines. These deceive and prime the natural immune system so that cancerous bio-targets induce a biological immune response that results in cancer elimination (therapeutic cancer vaccine) or cancer load reduction.

Sometimes a diseased body can be tricked into accepting an inherent cure. Gene therapy works on this principle whereby a gene or deoxyribonucleic acid (DNA) is the therapeutic agent used in combating disease. Two forms exist: (i) somatic gene therapy in which a therapeutic piece of DNA will be expressed in an individual who has a disease resulting from lack of or a defective segment of inherent DNA (this treatment will only last in the individual receiving the extraneous gene therapy), and (ii) germ-line gene therapy, in which DNA can be placed in germ lines, so that any defective or lacking genes will be negated by extraneous gene therapy for all subsequent replicative generations. Several vectors can be used in this genetic 'war on disease' through the application of both viral and nonviral vectors.

On occasion, what seems to be a beneficial gift to the body can be concurrently used as a cure. Oxygen is a prerequisite to life because of its energy-deriving effects in mitochondrial oxidative phosphorylation whereby adequate oxygen levels are favourably utilized to generate cellular energy. Some diseases such as cancer deviate from this preference in some instances to demonstrate a preference for energy in another format, namely the breakdown of cellular glucose into lactic acid through the process of glycolysis (named the Warburg Effect after Otto Heinrich Warburg [1883–1970] who won the 1931 Nobel Prize in physiology or medicine). Such a shift in metabolism may reflect a 'Janus effect' (from the two-headed Roman god of beginnings and transitions) of glucose metabolism in tumorigenesis. According to this paradigm, cancer cells initially favour standard oxidative energy derivation while actively inhibiting proglycolytic switches such as the energy-sensing enzyme AMP-activated protein kinase (AMPK); however, following cellular tumorigenesis progression, cancer cells demonstrate defective tumour suppressor status and progress to glycolytic switching for energy derivation to generate a selection advantage and growth. This Janus effect can be used to deceive cancer cells where beneficial oxygen in the form of hyperoxia (excessive oxygen partial pressures achieved through hyperbaric chambers) can be used to retard tumour growth, induce tumour cell death (through the release of toxic free radical and pro-inflammatory metabolites) by apoptosis, and even enhance anti-cancer chemotherapy.

Last, the body can be deceived into preventing disease. This can be achieved in preconditioning therapies, where the exposure of a minor insult to the body can induce a natural defence mechanism to prevent further disease, in a somewhat similar and yet different fashion to vaccines. In the example of ischaemic preconditioning, the short impairment of blood supply to an organ such as the heart can subsequently protect the heart against larger ischaemic insults such as coronary syndromes and myocardial infarctions. The mechanisms for this are considered to derive from inherent molecular humoural factors, which generate an early or classical phase of preconditioning (4–6 hours after an insult) and a longer secondary effect (24–72 hours after an insult).

19. Hence, when able to attack, we must seem unable; when using our forces, we must seem inactive; when we are near, we must make the enemy believe we are far away; when far away, we must make him believe we are near.

19. As diseases are not cognizant individuals we cannot react to them according to human emotional contexts. We can however personify disease in order to help our response to them.

(i) Hence when we have surgical tools, we must first consider the role of preventative medicine, which negated the need for unnecessary treatments and surgical invasiveness – 'prevention is therefore better than cure' – a concept first forwarded by the Roman-Etruscan poet Persius (Aulus Persius Flaccus 34–62 CE) in his statement to 'confront disease at its origins', *venienti occurrite morbo*. Another adage derived from the Roman and the pre-Roman eras includes *ubi pus, ibi evacua*, (where there is pus, it should be evacuated/drained). Of the most paramount importance is the principle *primum non nocere*: when considering a treatment it is vital to adhere to the concept of 'first (and primarily) do no harm.' While in reality most treatments, interventions and drugs carry side effects, this adage allows us to adopt a management plan for patients where the risk–benefit ratio is in favour of benefiting the patient, while also ensuring that patients are not subjected to unnecessary treatment risks in relation to the course and nature of the underlying pathology.

(ii) When using surgery and surgical force, we should first consider noninvasive and lower-risk treatment options. Performing no treatments can be an option if the risks of surgery and treatment are high. Each operation should be considered according to a risk-benefit judgement. As a result, surgery should only be offered to patients in cases where there is a failure or weakness of medical (and pharmacological) therapy or when surgery and medical therapy can provide the patient true benefits and improvements in health with the lowest possible risk of adverse events.

(iii) We should consider pharmacotherapy in depth, as the benefits of noninvasiveness can offer great safety and good patient outcomes. Clearly if pharmacotherapy is inadequate then surgery should be considered a treatment option. Just as in surgery, pharmacotherapies can act directly and indirectly. In pharmacotherapies, a drug binding to an active enzymatic ligand-binding site may bring about allosterism – a change in enzyme conformation and activity (direct allosterism). Alteration of the enzyme's activity also results from the drug binding on the enzyme away from the enzymatic ligand-binding site, changing the overall structure of the enzyme so that there is an alteration of enzyme activity and structure (indirect allosterism).

In surgery, there are many examples of direct and indirect procedures. Most procedures are direct – for example, an orthopaedic surgeon operates directly on the bone that is fractured, a cardiac surgeon operates directly on a diseased heart in open cardiac surgery and a colorectal surgeon directly removes a cancer from the colon. An example of indirect surgery would be the first procedures for cardiac angina, in which surgeons perform sub-total and total thyroidectomies to decrease systemic metabolic demand and hence cardiac output to decrease cardiac symptoms. Another example is bariatric surgery (also called metabolic surgery). Rather than offering simply weight loss through bypassing the bowel segments, these surgeries offer numerous multifaceted systematic effects on the whole body and its metabolism. As a result, although metabolic bariatric operations are performed directly on the gut, they achieve effects on the brain, kidney and heart through the entero-neuronal, entero-renal and entero-cardiac axes. The indirect operative value of these operations is immense, as they can resolve type 2 diabetes mellitus, leading to a bionic improvement in the body through the inherent manipulation of tissues (*autobionics*).

Indirect surgery can also result from indirect access to distant sites, and as a result surgeons can access different parts of the human body through distant but more appropriate or practical sites to minimize the footprint and invasiveness of surgery. One example is natural orifice transluminal endoscopic surgery (NOTES), in which access to the abdominal peritoneal cavity is achieved through the mouth and stomach or the vagina or anus rather than by making a direct incision on the anterior abdominal wall.

20. Hold out baits to entice the enemy. Feign disorder, and crush him.

20. Bait can be used to treat disease. Chemical bait can be used to attract and destroy disease parasites, and for surgical patients molecular baits offer added disease-attacking abilities. For example, Gla-domainless factor Xa can be used as a bait to bypass a blocked tenase complex in haemophilia, whereas many antibiotics such as the β-lactams can act as bait on bacterial cell walls to occupy crucial steps in development so as to result in bactericidal effects.

21. If he is secure at all points, be prepared for him. If he is in superior strength, evade him.

21. If there is significant metabolic disease, correct this pharmacotherapeutically and resuscitate the patient. If the source of disease is the cause for the disturbance and cannot be controlled medically, then excise the problem at the source. For example, in Graves disease the thyroid is responsible for systemic hyperthyroidism (increased metabolic rate, weight loss, gastrointestinal disturbance and neurological manifestations with weakness) as a result of an autoimmune increase in TSH- (thyroid-stimulating hormone/thyrotropin) receptor activation. This can be controlled by partial or complete removal of the thyroid gland.

22. If your opponent is of choleric temper, seek to irritate him. Pretend to be weak, that he may grow arrogant.

22. If the patient is pyrexial (has an elevated temperature), this can have negative side effects of systemic metabolism. Furthermore malignant hyperpyrexia can occur (typically due to anaesthetics) which can result in significant damage to all organs (including anaerobic metabolism and acidosis, massive deregulation of temperature-specific enzymes and widespread muscle injury and rigidity). These can be treated by pharmacotherapeutic anti-pyretics and treatment of the

underlying cause. If these fail, then surgical management with cardiopulmonary bypass to regulate temperature is an option to treat uncontrollable cases. Cardiopulmonary bypass can also be used to treat very low temperatures when severe and life-threatening hypothermia is not controlled by standard warming modalities.

23. If he is taking his ease, give him no rest. If his forces are united, separate them.

23. If the disease has a low stage it should nevertheless be treated with vigour. In cancers, for example, tumours are classified into stages and grades. Stages describe the level or severity of the tumour, established on elements including tumour location, number, dimensions and spread such as lymph nodes. Grades represent the severity of a cancer, usually based on components of tumour cell differentiation and ability to spread – a good analogy for this is a racing car on a race track representing a cancer cell. The stage of the cancer represents the distance the car has travelled on the racetrack, and the finish line represents the final stages of cancer and death of the body. The grade represents the engine and specifications of the car, where the higher the grade, the more powerful the engine, so the speed to the finish line – and ultimately death – is higher.

24. Attack him where he is unprepared, appear where you are not expected.

24. If disease processes are united, separate them. For example, synchronous (occurring at the same time) colorectal polyps should be excised, and there is evidence that synchronous colorectal cancer can be removed with good outcome (colon-colon or colon-liver metastasis). A patient with concomitant hypercholesterolaemia and coronary artery disease can have surgery for the coronary artery disease and continual medications for the hypercholesterolaemia, while a patient with concomitant coronary artery disease and valve disease should be considered for both to be treated surgically if the diseases are of adequate severity. This prevents both diseases from progressing and negates the need for and repeated risk of a second procedure. Selection for these cases should be rigorous, as double procedures can be more risky and carry higher mortality and morbidity (for example, a heart transplant carries certain risks that are increased if there is a concomitant lung and renal transplant). Sometimes hybrid procedures can be performed: for example, a robotic coronary artery bypass can take place on the left side of the heart (left anterior descending artery) and percutaneous interventions on the right side. A patient with surgical disease (such as cancer, vascular aneurysm or

cardiac disease) may have concomitant metabolic dysfunction of sepsis or shock. These patients need to be resuscitated (often in an intensive care setting) to manage their metabolic dysfunction before the surgical disease can be managed. This should always be considered for ill surgical patients.

It is also important to separate diseased tissues from healthy ones in order to target them more directly. This can be done by several mechanisms:

(i) Directly intraoperatively by physical separation of pathological tissue from surrounding tissues.

(ii) Intra-operative separation under electromechanical or visual guidance – for example the use of robotic surgery can offer 'augmented reality' by overlaying images of healthy and diseased tissue maps on the operative field so that a surgeon is guided through which areas are safe to incise and which areas of healthy tissue should be avoided.

(iii) Temporary separation during surgery – for example, in isolated limb perfusion (ILP) a diseased limb is separated from the systemic circulation via tourniquets, and the limb is given its own circulation artificially (using circulatory support and cardiovascular bypass perfusiontechnology). As a result, the diseased limb can receive isolated pharmacological chemotherapy, which will not enter the systemic circulation, so the patient will not become systemically unwell but will have the benefits of targeted therapy to a diseased portion of the body.

(iv) Separating a disease according to its molecular characteristics – for example, immune-based therapies targeting a disease process based on immunological epitopes and antibody-guided treatments.

(v) Separating a disease according to metabolic activity – for example, in photodynamic therapy, a photosensitizing agent (photo-sensitive drug) is preferentially taken up by the metabolic nature of some cancers. The uptake of such an agent will then render the cancerous tissue more prone to targeted therapy such as exposure to photonic energy and certain frequencies of light (including lasers) that can eradicate cancerous cells without damage to healthy tissues.

25. These military devices, leading to victory, must not be divulged beforehand.
25. These medical devices, leading to disease treatment and resolution, should not breed complacence.

26. Now the general who wins a battle makes many calculations in his temple ere the battle is fought. The general who loses a battle makes but few calculations beforehand. Thus do many calculations lead to victory, and few calculations to defeat: how much more no calculation at all! It is by attention to this point that I can foresee who is likely to win or lose.

26. Now the surgeon who succeeds in beating disease does so on decisions and computations based on the best evidence and medical knowledge, and the success of a treatment is achieved through this route. Surgeons with poor outcomes do not necessarily consider the background of the disease process and the patient's morbid status, pre-morbid condition and surgical anatomy. Thus consideration of physiology, biochemistry, pathology, anatomy and clinical integration leads to successful disease treatment, whereas not studying the patient's status before surgery can result in poor outcome and likely mortality. It is by attention to disease knowledge and best evidence that it can be foreseen who is likely to deliver successful life-saving surgery.

2 Performing Surgery

1. In the operations of war, where there are in the field a thousand swift chariots, as many heavy chariots, and a hundred thousand mail-clad soldiers, with provisions enough to carry them a thousand li, the expenditure at home and at the front, including entertainment of guests, small items such as glue and paint, and sums spent on chariots and armor, will reach the total of a thousand ounces of silver per day. Such is the cost of raising an army of 100,000 men.

1. When operating on a patient to combat disease, one should be aware of the operating theatre and its staff including surgical colleagues and juniors, anaesthetic staff, scrub nurses, operating room attendants and even the presence of medical and nursing students. Each operating theatre has an operating bed, surgical equipment that can range from a scalpel to a robot, anaesthetic equipment and specialist room ventilation.

There may be observers (medical and nonmedical) in an operating theatre and possibly industrial proctors (trainers). There would be theatre cleaning crew and hospital porters transporting patients in and out of the operating space. Such a complex setting has a commensurate financial cost of thousands of dollars or pounds sterling per day.

2. When you engage in actual fighting, if victory is long in coming, then men's weapons will grow dull and their ardor will be damped. If you lay siege to a town, you will exhaust your strength.

2. When you engage in surgery, if the procedure takes a long time, you prolong exposure of the patient to infection and excessive operative stress. Your equipment, such as blades or scalpels, may grow dull and require replacing. If your patient goes to an intensive therapy unit (ITU) the length of their stay typically follows a bimodal distribution, either brief or very prolonged. A long stay can weaken a patient's immune resources over a long period of time, and special consideration should be given to nutrition and immunomodulation for these patients.

3. Again, if the campaign is protracted, the resources of the State will not be equal to the strain.

3. If the disease process is protracted, the body will suffer from the strain; if the surgery is protracted, the patient will take a longer time to recover. If the surgery and hospital stay are protracted, the length of recovery and risk of complication can increase. Techniques designed to overcome delayed patient progress in the context of surgery include the design of enhanced recovery after surgery (ERAS) pathways that encourage early patient mobilization and prompt return to normal physiological status post-operatively.

4. Now, when your weapons are dulled, your ardor damped, your strength exhausted and your treasure spent, other chieftains will spring up to take advantage of your extremity. Then no man, however wise, will be able to avert the consequences that must ensue.

4. When surgical instruments are worn out, your pharmacotherapies expired, your energy wearied and your finances and medical supplies spent, diseases will continue to grow just as weeds take charge of a garden. When faced with such a situation no surgeon can avert the consequences of inadequate provisions, support and incentives.

5. Thus, though we have heard of stupid haste in war, cleverness has never been seen associated with long delays.

5. Although surgeons should be cognizant of undue operative haste, which can lead to surgical errors as a result of rushing, they must also consider that cleverness in surgery is not associated with long delays.

6. There is no instance of a country having benefited from prolonged warfare.

6. There is no instance that a patient has benefitted from unnecessarily long anaesthesia and unnecessarily long operations. Both carry side effects and must be applied judiciously according to appropriate risk–benefit considerations.

7. It is only one who is thoroughly acquainted with the evils of war that can thoroughly understand the profitable way of carrying it on.

7. Only those who comprehensively appreciate the side effects of surgery can thoroughly understand the beneficial way of performing it.

8. The skilful soldier does not raise a second levy, neither are his supply-wagons loaded more than twice.

8. The skilful surgeon does not use unnecessary tools and equipment, neither does he typically demand extra supplies (such as sutures or blood products) except in an unexpected or emergency situation.

9. Bring war material with you from home, but forage on the enemy. Thus the army will have food enough for its needs.

9. Use the patient's own native healing for operations. Closing wounds or suturing organs is a physical act of skilfully joining two tissues, but the patient's body does the majority of the work in completing this through the healing process. Therefore ensure your patient is well nourished. Apply the principle of autobionics where possible, in which a patient's own organs are used for the treatment of disease, as opposed to transplants of external materials (exobionics). This differentiation between auto- and exo-bionics is a modification of the term *bionics* (from the Greek: 'like life'), which was introduced by US Air Force Colonel Dr Jack E. Steele (1924–2009) in 1958. Of note, although Steele identified the paradigm of bionics as a reference to mankind's enhancement, the first concept of human enhancement was written over 4000 years ago in the Sumerian tale of *Lugalbanda and the Anzud Bird*. In this story the hero Lugalbanda gains the enhanced ability to physically travel the distance of seven mountains within a day. (The translation of the Sumerian text can be found at http://etcsl.orinst .ox.ac.uk/cgi-bin/etcsl.cgi?text = t.1.8.2.2#)

10. Poverty of the State exchequer causes an army to be maintained by contributions from a distance. Contributing to maintain an army at a distance causes the people to be impoverished.

10. A deterioration in national economic status is associated with a concomitant decline in national healthcare delivery that may affect the provision for surgery. As a result, total health expenditure is considered an important marker for national healthcare status and is a factor that is reported annually for every country by the World Bank as a percentage of gross domestic product (GDP).

11. On the other hand, the proximity of an army causes prices to go up; and high prices cause the people's substance to be drained away.

11. On the other hand, inefficient local healthcare expenditure can lead to depletion in national financial resources (such as GDP).

12. When their substance is drained away, the peasantry will be afflicted by heavy exactions.

12. Escalating uncontrolled healthcare costs can exhaust national expenditure in other areas.

13, 14. With this loss of substance and exhaustion of strength, the homes of the people will be stripped bare, and three-tenths of their income will be dissipated; while government expenses for broken chariots, worn-out horses, breast-plates and helmets, bows and arrows, spears and shields, protective mantles, draught-oxen and heavy wagons, will amount to four-tenths of its total revenue.

13, 14. Well-managed healthcare expenditure is vital to a national economy and is therefore an important consideration for governments, politicians, and patients as well as healthcare practitioners and surgeons.

15. Hence a wise general makes a point of foraging on the enemy. One cartload of the enemy's provisions is equivalent to twenty of one's own, and likewise a single picul of his provender is equivalent to twenty from one's own store.

15. Hence a wise surgeon makes a point of understanding disease processes and their treatments. It is vital to adhere to an evidence-based practice to achieve healthcare quality and value. Institutions such as the United Kingdom's National Institute for Health and Care Excellence (NICE) are aimed at supporting optimal clinical decision-making in addition to providing knowledge regarding the relative and absolute cost-effectiveness of various treatments.

16. Now in order to kill the enemy, our men must be roused to anger; that there may be advantage from defeating the enemy, they must have their rewards.

16. Now in order to defeat diseases, surgeons must be motivated so that there may be advantage from defeating the disease, and so that the patients may derive a decent quality of life (as opposed to only life or death) and enhanced well-being.

17. Therefore in chariot fighting, when ten or more chariots have been taken, those should be rewarded who took the first. Our own flags should be substituted for those of the enemy, and the chariots mingled and used in conjunction with ours. The captured soldiers should be kindly treated and kept.

17. Therefore in cancer surgery, tissue samples should be taken and sent to histology for diagnostic staging and grading. However, these tissues should be explanted to allow healing and patient recovery at an individual level. Further study of these explanted tissues can be used for cellular and molecular analyses for insights regarding disease mechanisms, and the study of tissues from many sources can give information regarding population trends in disease progression.

18. This is called, using the conquered foe to augment one's own strength.

18. This is called research, where the mechanistic study of disease can increase medical knowledge and generate efficacious treatments.

19. In war, then, let your great object be victory, not lengthy campaigns.

19. In surgery, then, let your great object be victory over disease, not lengthy operations. Unnecessarily lengthy procedures and overly long anaesthetic times can have result in consequences for the patient.

20. Thus it may be known that the leader of armies is the arbiter of the people's fate, the man on whom it depends whether the nation shall be in peace or in peril.

20. Thus it may be known that surgeons can be the arbiters of the people's diseases, the ones on whom it depends whether the nation shall be in health or disease.

3 Surgical Strategies

1. In the practical art of war, the best thing of all is to take the enemy's country whole and intact; to shatter and destroy it is not so good. So, too, it is better to recapture an army entire than to destroy it, to capture a regiment, a detachment or a company entire than to destroy them.

1. In the practical art of surgery, the best thing to do is to manage the complete disease process where possible. For example in metabolic surgery, performing a bariatric procedure should be just one facet of a broader approach to the patient's eating behaviour, exercise and lifestyle environment and concurrent management of other co-morbidities such as diabetes and sleep apnoea. In this way, the overall route to a patient having improved quality of life, health and well-being will be maximized. Simply performing the surgery without addressing all the other disease aspects will diminish surgical benefits. It is not much good to perform

an operation when the underlying disease process has not been addressed so that it will recur to cause more pathology (except in some cases of palliation, where de-bulking a tumour may offer an increase in symptom-free time). In cancers, the best thing of all is to remove the tumour whole and intact without disturbing its tissues or its surroundings. This decreases tumour seeding and local tissue trauma. In addition, it is important to recognize that combating one facet of cancer disease alone may result in its compensating to increase its severity through other mechanisms. For example, in some breast cancers, inhibition of the integrin receptors will result in a compensatory activation of a pro-metastatic switch. Similarly, an incomplete or insufficient approach to using antibiotics for infectious disease and bacterial sepsis will lead to the unwanted effects of antibiotic resistance, whose problems have escalated at a global level.

2. Hence to fight and conquer in all your battles is not supreme excellence; supreme excellence consists in breaking the enemy's resistance without fighting.

2. Hence the performance of surgery on all patients is not supreme excellence; supreme excellence consists in treating disease with the least possible surgical footprint, without patients undergoing any unnecessary surgical trauma.

3. Thus the highest form of generalship is to balk the enemy's plans; the next best is to prevent the junction of the enemy's forces; the next in order is to attack the enemy's army in the field; and the worst policy of all is to besiege walled cities.

3. The highest form of medical leadership is to achieve disease eradication (demonstrated in the case of smallpox); the next best is disease prevention (typically through disease awareness and education including examples of enhancing diet and lifestyle measures, applying universal precautions of hygiene and minimizing disease exposure); the next best is to treat disease directly through surgery or medical pharmacotherapy; and the most unfortunate scenario is where disease prognosis cannot be changed so that supportive and palliative measures must be engaged to optimize quality of life.

There is also the paradigm of *divide and conquer* enemies which was derived from the father of Alexander the Great, Philip II of Macedon (382–336 BCE) [διαίρει καὶ βασίλευε/*divide et impera*] and Gaius Julius Caesar (100–44 BCE) [*divide ut regnes*]. This can be applied in healthcare where some diseases have been purposely applied to patients to combat another disease. For example, malaria inoculation therapy was used to treat tertiary syphilis (which ultimately resulted in the awarding of a Nobel Prize in physiology or medicine to the Austrian physician Julius

Wagner-Jauregg [1857–1940] in 1927). In addition, in the time of Hippocrates, it was noticed that some patients with neurological disease recovered after an illness when there was a pyrexial or temperature-inducing element. This highlights an evolutionary stepping-stone in our scientific innovation to combat infectious diseases.

Applying a 'disease-against-disease' archetype is distinct from vaccine biology (in which infectious agents are applied to generate immune defence) in that it reveals a multilateral interplay whereby infectious agents demonstrate a biological dialogue with other infectious agents. As a result, the infectious agents are not purely pathogenic to a single host in a binary manner, but, depending on their biocompetitive environment, demonstrate 'fuzzy pathogenesis' (or relative degrees of pathogenicity).

Malaria is a pertinent example of fuzzy pathogenesis, as it displays therapeutic activity on syphilis, while conversely its own pathogenesis can be diminished by other parasites (including *Ascaris lumbricoides* and the *Schistosoma* spp.).

The ancient doctrine of 'the enemy of my enemy is my friend' holds true in biology, and an increased understanding of such fuzzy pathogenesis mechanisms may contribute to the next generation of innovative new treatments for global communicable diseases.

4. The rule is, not to besiege walled cities if it can possibly be avoided. The preparation of mantlets, movable shelters, and various implements of war, will take up three whole months; and the piling up of mounds over against the walls will take three months more.

4. The rule is not to have the patient require intensive care therapy if it can possibly be avoided. The preparation of airway tools, ventilation machines, anti-bedsore mattresses, anaesthetic pharmacotherapies, nursing and medical staff requires significant time and energy, and more importantly represents an increased likelihood of protracted patient recovery time.

5. The general, unable to control his irritation, will launch his men to the assault like swarming ants, with the result that one-third of his men are slain, while the town still remains untaken. Such are the disastrous effects of a siege.

5. The surgeon unable to control his emotions may unwittingly launch into a difficult operation with unnecessary manoeuvres that may result in unnecessary tissue damage, poor patient outcomes and ultimately a lower quality of care.

6. Therefore the skillful leader subdues the enemy's troops without any fighting; he captures their cities without laying siege to

them; he overthrows their kingdom without lengthy operations
in the field.

6. Therefore the skilful surgeon can subdue disease with
minimal invasiveness to the patient, and where possible
without needing to operate; he or she can utilize non-
surgical modalities such as disease prevention policies, or
target disease processes with pharmacotherapy, chemotherapy and sometimes behavioural therapy without having to
expose the patient to surgery.

7. With his forces intact he will dispute the mastery of the
Empire, and thus, without losing a man, his triumph will
be complete. This is the method of attacking by stratagem.

7. Without having to make utility of surgical staff, equipment and hospital resources the surgeon can negate any
unnecessary surgical risks. Adopting a staged approach
of applying surgical therapy only when lower-risk non-
surgical strategies have been applied and shown not to be
adequately efficacious is the method to apply surgery.*

17. Thus we may know that there are five essentials for victory:
(1) He will win who knows when to fight and when not to

---

* Points 8 to 16 have been excluded as a medical metaphor is not directly applicable.

fight. (2) He will win who knows how to handle both superior and inferior forces. (3) He will win whose army is animated by the same spirit throughout all its ranks. (4) He will win who, prepared himself, waits to take the enemy unprepared. (5) He will win who has military capacity and is not interfered with by the sovereign.

17. Thus we may know that there are five essentials for surgical success:

(1) He will win who knows when to operate or when not to operate.

(2) He will win who understands how to interact and manage colleagues and team members of different skills, strengths and aptitudes. How to speak to anaesthetists, nurses, and junior and senior staff is critical for successful surgery. At a practical level the same concept applies to the actual craft of surgery where tissue handling – manipulating tissues according to their tensile strength and disease load – is of vital importance for operative success.

(3) He will win whose surgical team is animated by the same spirit throughout all its ranks.

(4) He will win who prepared himself and has studied the disease process and the patient undergoing

surgical treatment so that the patient receives an
operation ultimately suited to him or her.

(5) He will win who has objective surgical decisions
guided by the best evidence and information (personalized and precision evidence-based medicine).

18. Hence the saying: If you know the enemy and know your-
self, you need not fear the result of a hundred battles. If you
know yourself but not the enemy, for every victory gained
you will also suffer a defeat. If you know neither the enemy nor
yourself, you will succumb in every battle.

18. Hence if you appreciate the disease process and truly
know your own skills and those of your team, you should
be well placed to make a decision as to whether to operate
safely. If you know yourself but are not fully aware of disease characteristics, such as surgical anatomy, patient medical characteristics (e.g. diabetes, past medical history, drug
history) or tumour stage and grade, then surgical outcomes
may be profoundly poor. As the surgeon, if you know neither the disease process nor yourself, you will succumb in
every operation.

4 Surgical Decision Making

1. The good fighters of old first put themselves beyond the possibility of defeat, and then waited for an opportunity of defeating the enemy.

1. A strong motivation and mental attitude are paramount to successfully combat disease. It is also critical to study medical history and the evidence generated from previous medical research and literature ('good surgeons of old').

The first description of medical symptoms in history is recorded as fevers associated with shaking chills and severe headaches which are common to a myriad of differential diagnoses (including viral or bacterial causes). According to the Sumerian legend of *Lugalbanda in the Mountain Cave* written in the 21st century BCE, the story's hero Lugalbanda falls sick for two days, suffering from severe headache, rigors and chills:

Head sickness befell him. He jerked like a snake dragged by its head with a reed; his mouth bit the dust, like a gazelle caught in a snare. No longer could his hands return the hand grip, no longer could he lift his feet high . . . his teeth chattered (http://etcsl.orinst.ox.ac.uk/section1/tr1821.htm).

This 4000-year-old description written in cuneiform was composed at approximately the same time as the *Sumerian Therapeutic Manual*, which corresponds to the ancient Ur III period. While the manual is considered to be the first medical treatise in history, it does not offer diagnoses or descriptors of symptomatology noted in the Lugalbanda's legend. The recognition of the similar symptoms that bridge a 4000-year period identifies a common thread of pathology that has afflicted mankind. It also serves to reinforce the sophistication of disease classification of the ancient world.

2. To secure ourselves against defeat lies in our own hands, but the opportunity of defeating the enemy is provided by the enemy himself.

2. To secure ourselves against surgical failure lies in our own hands, but the opportunity of defeating disease is provided by the disease itself.

3. Thus the good fighter is able to secure himself against defeat, but cannot make certain of defeating the enemy.

3. Thus the good surgeon is able to secure himself against surgical mishaps and can increase patient safety, but cannot make certain of defeating disease.

4. Hence the saying: One may know how to conquer without being able to do it.

4. Hence one may know how to conquer disease without being able to do it. The responsible surgeon does the utmost to prevent surgical mistakes and studies disease pathology to cure illness.

5. Security against defeat implies defensive tactics; ability to defeat the enemy means taking the offensive.

5. Security against disease implies defensive tactics through prevention; ability to defeat disease means taking the offensive through surgery and active medical treatment.

6. Standing on the defensive indicates insufficient strength; attacking, a superabundance of strength.

6. Standing on the defensive indicates forethought and allows a preventative strategy; attacking a disease implies

that active medications and operations are available for use in treating patients.

7. The general who is skilled in defense hides in the most secret recesses of the earth; he who is skilled in attack flashes forth from the topmost heights of heaven. Thus on the one hand we have ability to protect ourselves; on the other, a victory that is complete.

7. The doctor who is skilled in preventative medicine studies epidemiological trends and can readily determine association and causation based on the Bradford Hill criteria (named after Sir Austin Bradford Hill FRS [1897–1991] who describes these in 1965). These include (a) temporal relationship (which by itself can be used to derive causation 'of sorts' through Sir Clive Granger's [1934–2009] causality test for which he was awarded the 2003 Nobel Memorial Prize in economic sciences); (b) strengthen usually quantified by odds ratios or relative risks; (c) dose-response relationship; (d) consistency; (e) plausibility; (f) consideration of alternate explanations through analogy; (g) experimental evidence with reversibility; (h) specificity; and (i) coherence (fits in with current theory). He who is skilled in surgery applies this modality to ensure timely patient treatment.

Thus on the one hand we have ability to protect ourselves, and on the other, a victory against disease may be complete.

A mnemonic for Bradford Hill causality is:

Dr Strong ACCEPTS

Dr – Dose response (biological gradient)

Strong (Strength)

A – Analogy (or alternate explanations excluded)

C – Consistency

C – Coherence (fits in with current theory)

E – Experimental evidence

P – Plausible

T – Temporality

S – Specificity

8. To see victory only when it is within the ken of the common herd is not the acme of excellence.

8. To see victory in treating disease only when it is within the ken of general belief is not the acme of excellence in combating disease and achieving quality. The key is to offer value and quality while encouraging innovation.

9. Neither is it the acme of excellence if you fight and conquer and the whole Empire says, 'Well done!'

9. Neither is it the acme of excellence if you fight and conquer disease for all your colleagues to say, 'Well done!'

10. To lift an autumn hair is no sign of great strength; to see the sun and moon is no sign of sharp sight; to hear the noise of thunder is no sign of a quick ear.

10. Diagnosing a tension pneumothorax on an X-ray is no sign of great strength (this should have been diagnosed and treated clinically without the need for an X-ray); to make a diagnosis based on the report of a radiological scan is no sign of sharp sight (for someone else has done the work for you); to hear the dysphonia and dysphagia of epiglottitis is no sign of a quick ear, nor is picking up Hamman's crunch sign of pneumo-mediastinum. While these signs are associated with underlying diseases, they represent advanced disease status and earlier signs should have been primarily diagnosed well in advance of these. There is no room to be complacent as a surgeon.

11. What the ancients called a clever fighter is one who not only wins, but excels in winning with ease.

11. What the great surgeons called a clever surgeon is one who not only successfully treats patients, but also excels in surgery with ease.

12. Hence his victories bring him neither reputation for wisdom nor credit for courage.

12. Hence his surgical successes bring him neither reputation for wisdom nor credit for courage.

13. He wins his battles by making no mistakes. Making no mistakes is what establishes the certainty of victory, for it means conquering an enemy that is already defeated.

13. He achieves operative success by minimizing mistakes and enhancing surgery. Making no mistakes is what establishes an increased likelihood for operative success, for it means conquering a disease according to sound surgical principles.

14. Hence the skilful fighter puts himself into a position which makes defeat impossible, and does not miss the moment for defeating the enemy.

14. Hence the skilful surgeon puts himself into a position which maximizes patient safety and minimizes patient risk while optimizing successful health outcomes.

15. Thus it is that in war the victorious strategist only seeks battle after the victory has been won, whereas he who is destined to defeat first fights and afterwards looks for victory.

15. Thus it is that in surgery the victorious strategist only seeks an operation after the patient has been physiologically optimized. This means adequate fluid resuscitation, complete medical control of systemic conditions such as diabetes and pre-operative nutritional enhancement. He who is destined to poor surgical outcomes operates without consideration of the patient's complete medical background.

16. The consummate leader cultivates the moral law, and strictly adheres to method and discipline; thus it is in his power to control success.

16. The consummate surgeon cultivates patient ethics, and strictly adheres to surgical methods and discipline; thus it is in his power to control success.

17. In respect of military method, we have, firstly, Measurement; secondly, Estimation of quantity; thirdly, Calculation; fourthly, Balancing of chances; fifthly, Victory.

17. In respect of the surgical method, we have, firstly, measurement (of outcomes); second, estimation of quantity (number of subjects and frequency of pathology); third, calculation (of operative success); fourth, balancing of chances (probabilities and risk–benefit ratios); and fifth, selection of the best surgical strategy to achieve victory against disease.

18. Measurement owes its existence to Earth; Estimation of quantity to Measurement; Calculation to Estimation of quantity; Balancing of chances to Calculation; and Victory to Balancing of chances.

18. Measurement of outcomes owes its existence to surgical research and audit; estimation of quantity to measurement; calculation to estimation of quantity; balancing of chances to calculation; and victory to balancing of chances.

Archibald Pitcairne (1652–1713), the Scottish physician, can be credited as introducing the practice of utilizing advanced mathematical methodology in modern medicine. He had an established dialogue with the great mathematician and physicist Isaac Newton (1642–1727) and later described the application of mathematics in medicine through the paradigm of Iatromathematics. Today these effects can be seen in the empiricism of clinical research studies, the computational methods of bioinformatics, integration of data in medical imaging modalities and identification of the Fibonacci golden-ratio patterns in human embryology (such as those of coronary artery anatomy) or of vascular patterns in the lumina and surface epithelia of the gastrointestinal tract.

19. A victorious army opposed to a routed one, is as a pound's weight placed in the scale against a single grain.

19. A victorious surgeon can be likened to a targeted force annihilating disease. Hence the special forces metaphor that a successful military operation is akin to the surgical excision of a cancer.

20. The onrush of a conquering force is like the bursting of pent-up waters into a chasm a thousand fathoms deep.

20. The onrush of a conquering surgical force is like that of ninjas storming a castle in order to disempower, comprehensively remove and defeat a disease. The metaphor of surgery defeating pathology akin to special military forces defeating their foe goes both ways – some special forces personnel liken themselves to surgeons excising cancers with precision.

5 Operative Methodology

1. The control of a large force is the same principle as the control of a few men: it is merely a question of dividing up their numbers.

1. The control of a large disease lesion is the same principle as the control of a small one: it is merely a question of dividing up the lesion into smaller resectable pieces (although sometimes it is advisable to remove some lesions such as cancers with their tissue wall intact to prevent seeding). The problem of managing a complex multifactorial disease is addressed in a similar manner, by dividing it into smaller manageable pieces. The world of computers also applies this methodology, called 'decomposition' or 'factoring' in which a complex problem can be addressed through the management of smaller components of the bigger issue.

2. Fighting with a large army under your command is nowise different from fighting with a small one: it is merely a question of instituting signs and signals.

2. Operating with a large surgical team under your leadership in the context of a complex operation should not be conceptually different from performing minor operations with local anaesthesia. The principle should incorporate patient safety, universal precautions and excellent communication among all team members to offer optimal patient care. The difference in a larger operation is merely a question of instituting appropriate communication channels such as those with surgical colleagues, anaesthetists, scrub staff and operating theatre assistants.

3. To ensure that your whole host may withstand the brunt of the enemy's attack and remain unshaken – this is effected by maneuvers direct and indirect.

3. To ensure optimal surgical outcomes, it is necessary to strengthen all surgical modalities to minimize the effects of disease processes. This requires consideration of direct and indirect surgical manoeuvres. Direct surgery includes actual operating whereas indirect surgery can be divided into intra-operative and extra-operative components (see Chapter 1).

Intra-operative factors include ergonomics, setting up the case, patient position (for example, lithotomy position), the appropriate use of arm boards, patient warming blankets, anti-thrombotic calf-compression boots and tissue retractors. Intra-operative factors also include technical elements such as setting up your assistant to help and retract adequately. In laparoscopic surgery, your assistant may be your 'camera man'. Laparoscopic surgery is 'all about your left hand' implying that most surgeons operate with a dominant right hand to make incisions, ties and sutures. The non-dominant left hand is usually used to retract and expose tissue; the work of the dominant hand can only take place when the non-dominant supports it, much in the way that a ying has a yang. Indirect intra-operative factors also play an important role and include the surgeon's style of team leadership, how he or she communicates, directs, motivates and incentivizes the team. All these factors can act together to affect patient outcomes.

Extra-operative factors include the patient's resuscitation status, and if there was a need for pre- or post-operative medications such as adjuvant (post-operative) and neo-adjuvant (pre-operative) radiotherapy or chemotherapy. Other factors also include post-operative care. Will the patient be managed in the high-dependency unit (HDU), intensive care unit (ICU) or ward setting? Should the patient be mobilized early; should the patient undergo enhanced recovery strategies? All of these factors will contribute to patient outcome and if done properly can contribute to the success of the procedure.

4. That the impact of your army may be like a grindstone dashed against an egg – this is effected by the science of weak points and strong.

4. That the impact of your surgical team on a disease process may be like a sledgehammer crushing an egg – in the context of disease pathology, this is effected by the science of understanding each disease's specific pathological strengths and weaknesses so that they can be targeted for treatment.

5. In all fighting, the direct method may be used for joining battle, but indirect methods will be needed in order to secure victory.

5. In all surgery, the direct method may be used for performing operations, but indirect methods will be needed to secure victory against disease.

6. Indirect tactics, efficiently applied, are inexhaustible as Heaven and Earth, unending as the flow of rivers and streams;

like the sun and moon, they end but to begin anew; like the four seasons, they pass away to return once more.

6. Indirect surgical tactics are an eternal mainstay of treatment. This includes the constant monitoring and management of patients to resuscitate them physiologically at all times. The steadfastness of physiological optimization is akin to a constant circle of care that enhances all aspects of healthcare.

7. There are not more than five musical notes, yet the combinations of these five give rise to more melodies than can ever be heard.

7. There are a finite number of surgical incision types, but applying them in different anatomies, pathologies and tissue settings gives rise to a vast number of possible operations.

8. There are not more than five primary colours (blue, yellow, red, white, and black), yet in combination they produce more hues than can ever been seen.

8. There are not more than five primary colours (blue, yellow, red, white, and black), yet in combination they produce more hues than can ever been seen. The great polymath Thomas Young (1773–1829), a prominent decipherer of the hieroglyphs and initiator of the wave theory of light, also

developed the trichromatic theory of colour vision (Young–
Helmholtz theory) specifying that we actually interpret all
colours based on the sensing of three primary colours red,
green and blue, or the RGB colour model.

*9. There are not more than five cardinal tastes (sour, acrid,
salt, sweet, bitter), yet combinations of them yield more fla-
vours than can ever be tasted.*

9. There is a quantifiable number of surgical approaches:
open, minimally invasive, endoscopic, microsurgical,
robotic and so on, and so for each patient the possibility of
a highly bespoke procedure can be achieved. Such a variation depends on local availability of technology and care
support, surgical and technical education and expertise,
surgical and patient choice, all within the context of the
drivers of local healthcare practice.

*10. In battle, there are not more than two methods of attack:
the direct and the indirect; yet these two in combination give
rise to an endless series of maneuvers.*

10. In surgery, there are not more than two methods of
operating – the direct and the indirect (see Chapter 1), yet
these two in combination give rise to an endless series of
surgical manoeuvres.

11. The direct and the indirect lead on to each other in turn. It is like moving in a circle – you never come to an end. Who can exhaust the possibilities of their combination?

11. Direct and indirect surgical manoeuvres complement each other; surgical success is highly efficacious when a patient's care derives from the optimal and balanced concurrent application of both direct and indirect strategies.

12. The onset of troops is like the rush of a torrent which will even roll stones along in its course.

12. The onset of surgery through the surgical team is akin to the propagation of momentum and dynamism seen in a landslide or avalanche of targeted surgical power; when applied in a correct setting and when galvanized appropriately, disease survival and persistence can be negated by an impenetrably powerful surgical force.

13. The quality of decision is like the well-timed swoop of a falcon which enables it to strike and destroy its victim.

13. The quality of a surgical decision in the management of disease is like the well-timed swoop of a falcon, which enables it to strike and prevent the progression of disease that could otherwise result in the death of its victim.

14. Therefore the good fighter will be terrible in his onset, and prompt in his decision.

14. Therefore the good surgeon will be robust in his or her approach in diminishing and overcoming disease processes, while judicious and prompt in his or her surgical decision making.

15. Energy may be likened to the bending of a crossbow; decision, to the releasing of a trigger.

15. Surgical energy may be likened to pulling a crossbow (gaining diagnostic information), making a decision to operate (according to the best evidence) and releasing the trigger – performing the operation with the highest surgical precision.

16. Amid the turmoil and tumult of battle, there may be seeming disorder and yet no real disorder at all; amid confusion and chaos, your array may be without head or tail, yet it will be proof against defeat.

16. Amid the turmoil and tumult of surgery, there may seem to be disorder to an outsider watching the operation and yet no real disorder at all; the multifactorial events in an operation may depict chaos and haphazard events. Removing a complex fungating tumour or repairing a complex aneurysm may demonstrate aesthetic pleasure,

although the pathology does not typically offer this. A good surgeon has control of the operative steps and strategy and should be supported by a well-disciplined and effective team so that the proof will be in the patient cure.

17. Simulated disorder postulates perfect discipline, simulated fear postulates courage; simulated weakness postulates strength.
17. Simulation in surgery postulates perfect discipline, simulated fear postulates surgical safety, and simulated weakness postulates surgical preparedness. Simulations can offer short learning curves, improved surgical confidence, increased patient safety and enhanced patient outcomes. Surgical simulations were used as early as the time of Sushruta in the sixth century BCE, when procedures would be practised on vegetables and inanimate objects before being performed on human subjects. Today's surgical simulators have an increased level of precision, with powerful electronic capabilities to help the next generation of surgeons practise both technical and non-technical skills while also offering the ability to assess the surgical practitioners of the future. Simulators offer training in open, minimally invasive (laparoscopic and thoracoscopic) and robotic surgery and can also help train anaesthetists and other theatre staff at their tasks. They can also be used to

teach medical students basic surgical procedures such as patient resuscitation and suturing.

18. Hiding order beneath the cloak of disorder is simply a question of subdivision; concealing courage under a show of timidity presupposes a fund of latent energy; masking strength with weakness is to be effected by tactical dispositions.

18. 'Deception' against disease should be applied where possible. Examples include molecular mimicry, the β-lactam antibiotic family, bionics (including auto-bionics), gene therapy, hyperoxia and preconditioning.

19. Thus one who is skillful at keeping the enemy on the move maintains deceitful appearances, according to which the enemy will act. He sacrifices something that the enemy may snatch at it.

19. Thus one who is skilful at applying all therapies, be they direct or 'deceptive to the disease', can offer a wide and successful arsenal in the struggle against pathology.

20. By holding out baits, he keeps him on the march; then with a body of picked men he lies in wait for him.

20. The surgeon must therefore think laterally and brainstorm where appropriate to offer the best treatment for patients. While *Primum non nocere* (first, do no harm)

must be adhered to, an open mind to all sources of information may offer novel therapies that can lead to improved patient outcomes.

21. The clever combatant looks to the effect of combined energy, and does not require too much from individuals. Hence his ability to pick out the right men and utilize combined energy.
21. The clever surgeon looks to the effect of combined energy, and does not require too much from individuals. Hence his ability to pick out the right team members and utilize combined energy.

22. When he utilizes combined energy, his fighting men become as it were like unto rolling logs or stones. For it is the nature of a log or stone to remain motionless on level ground, and to move when on a slope; if four-cornered, to come to a standstill, but if round-shaped, to go rolling down.
22. When he utilizes combined energy, the skills and knowledge of the whole team are integrated and galvanized to more than the sum of its parts when combating disease. The whole team acts as a multifaceted weapon against pathology, all their energy guided and streamlined to achieve the ultimate goal of enhancing patient outcomes, quality of care and well-being.

23. Thus the energy developed by good fighting men is as the momentum of a round stone rolled down a mountain thousands of feet in height. So much on the subject of energy.

23. Thus the energy developed by a good surgical team offers great momentum to battle against the disease process. The strength of cohesion, teamwork and knowledge in this team is reflected in the effectiveness of an operation and ultimately enhances surgical outcome.

6 Civilization

1. In war, the general receives his commands from the sovereign.
1. In healthcare, the surgeon takes his inspiration to achieve patient quality of life and well-being from civilization. At a practical level he is guided by the rules and regulations offered by national/international healthcare policy, healthcare institutional leadership and best evidence.

The definition of civilization has been among the most prominent questions of mankind and remains as relevant to surgeons as it does society as a whole. The term *civilization* derives from the Latin *civilis* that relates to citizenship and public or political life, although in the modern era this term carries a broader and more powerful connotation than the Oxford Dictionary's definition as 'the process by which a society or place reaches an advanced stage of social development and organization'.[1] Defining an objective measure of such a concept has for many centuries been a source of unfulfilled endeavour by multitudes of scientists, philosophers and global scholars, and a universally accepted standard for civilization has remained elusive.

It is widely accepted that some of the earliest evidence of civilization took place in the so-called 'cradle of civilization' in the 'Fertile Crescent' of the Ancient Near East, circa 6500 to 3800 BCE.[2] The birth of civilization there coincided directly with the introduction of early mathematical principles and tools that were most frequently associated with application to economic and financial transactions (land ownership, farming and trade). Since that time the role of finances and economics on civilization has received a disapproving press in the current worldwide climate, where financial meltdowns and booms dominate global decisions. The contribution of the world's financial status to the state of human society and civilization is nevertheless undeniable. Even luminaries of economics agree on the association between monetary standing and civilization; John Maynard Keynes (1883–1946) specified that 'economics and economists are the trustees not of civilisation, but the possibility of civilisation' (Roy Harrod, The Life of John Maynard Keynes, *The Economic Journal*, Vol. 61, No. 242, June, 1951, pp. 372–376), and Friedrich

August Hayek (1899–1992) considered that the free market was intimately associated with civilization.

The determinants of societal growth and advancement are also powerfully linked to the application of available energy. Whether in the form of oil, coal, nuclear or other industrial energy supply, societies universally require energy to fuel life, transport, trade and communication. In this context the Soviet radio astronomer Nikolai Kardashev proposed a scale in 1964 to define civilization based on its energy consumption. This had initially been intended as a practical and quantifiable measure of civilization using established radio-astronomical tools that were available at the time to assess extraterrestrial civilizations (Table 6.1), but has been recently adapted by popular scientists intraterrestrially to assess the status of human civilization based

Table 6.1 The Modified Kardashev Scale

Civilization Level	Magnitude of Energy Utilization	Kardashev's Proposed Energy Consumption
I	Entire planet	4×10^{12} watts
II	Entire star	4×10^{26} watts
III	Entire galaxy	4×10^{37} watts
IV	Entire super-cluster	
V	Entire universe	
VI	Entire multi-verse	

Note: Levels I through III were proposed by Nikolai Kardashev in 1964 and Levels IV through VI were added later by other authors.

on global energy consumption. Carl Sagan further proposed that the levels of consumption in the scale should be modified to accommodate an order of magnitude difference between classes such that a civilization Type 1.7 consumes 10^{23} watts, and a civilization Type 2.3 consumes 10^{29} watts. According to current approximations defined by Sagan ($K = (\text{Log } W - 6)/10$), mankind can be calculated to be a class 0.72 civilization, with the prediction that we shall achieve a fully fledged level 1 civilization within the coming centuries.

Applying the Kardashev scale to mankind can also offer the study of its trend that is directly derived from global energy consumption data. It is notable that the trend in global energy consumption very closely resembles the trend in global finances demonstrated through the element of global gross domestic product (GDP) (Figure 6.1a). Consequently there is a high concordance in the trend of global Kardashev score and global GDP (Figure 6.1b).

The association of modified Kardashev civilization score and GDP can be termed the 'Civilomic' score and allows us to calculate the level of civilization according to economics and market dynamics (Figure 6.1c). It reflects the ancient association between civilization and economics, but importantly can give us an accurate and

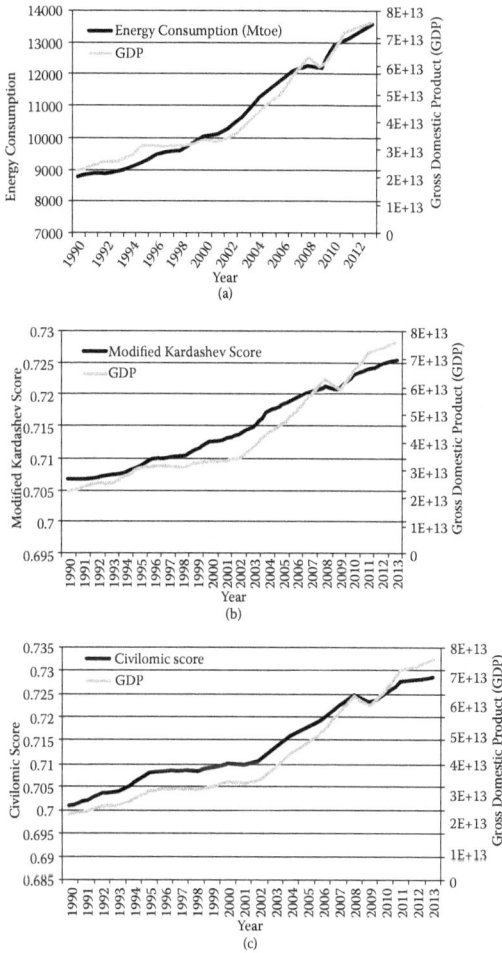

Figure 6.1 Global trends in (a) energy consumption (Enderdata) and GDP (World Bank). (b) Civilization score by the modified Kardashev score (derived from Enerdata and Sagan's formula) and GDP. (c) Civilization score by the Civilomic score and GDP. Note: [#]E + 13: the value × 10 to the power of 13.

objective estimate of our current civilization level based on regularly reported fiscal values. There is some evidence of causality between energy and economic growth, where aggregate energy consumption to GDP and GDP to energy consumption is more prevalent in the developed OECD (Organisation for Economic Co-operation and Development) countries compared to the developing non-OECD countries. The proposed application of GDP to a modified Kardashev civilization scale through Civilomics has importance as the value of GDP can be calculated by three accepted methods (production, expenditure and income), which can offer a mechanistic breakdown of why GDP increases or decreases (Figure 6.2). Studying our level of civilization through Civilomics (and therefore GDP) can therefore identify individual mechanistic societal factors that can alter our calculated level of civilization. For example, what is the effect of global government spending, international trade, taxation and investment on the proposed score as a civilization? The current understanding of GDP is more versatile than absolute energy consumption scores. Analysing the modified Kardashev score in this context cannot only modify global financial strategies but also offers unique political policy insights in addition to generating new economical models and societal knowledge. It is

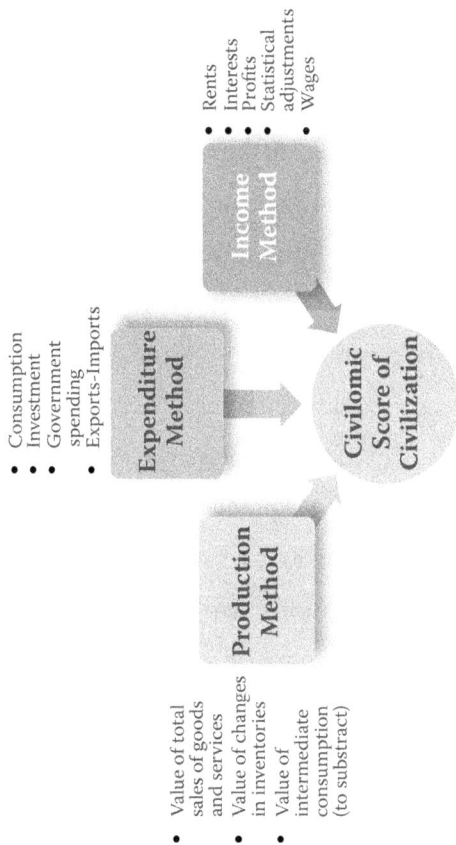

Figure 6.2 The Civilomic score of civilization derived through the calculation GDP/Modified Kardashev Score and its contributory variables.

important to note that just as the Kardashev scale applies to global energy consumption, the Civilomic score derives from global GDP and therefore applying its calculation to a single nation state would not offer a representative measure of civilization for that individual state; rather it is a measure of worldwide civilization.

There is, however, discord between the global GDP forecasts which predict modest-to-weak short-term growth (International Monetary Fund's *World Economic Outlook* [IMF-WEO]), and those of global energy consumption described in the International Energy Agency's (IEA) 'business as usual' scenario and the Intergovernmental Panel on Climate Change (IPCC) A1FI scenario, where a strong rise in energy consumption is predicted. It is likely that the path of civilization will follow the balances that guide both the global economy and world energy consumption so that there may be a possibility to modify their contributory elements leading to societal progress.

The benefits of quantifying civilization through economic markets include the reality that many economic trends can be explained through large-scale human behaviour. Changes in global stock prices can be reflective of short- and long-term human judgments and decisions. This unearths the role of individual human psychologies impacting economic choices through behavioural economics. For example, wars and global infectious diseases carry a major impact on global stock prices and as a result global finances undergo cycles of 'agony' and 'ecstasy'. Many individual stock prices vary according to the confidence they incur on their shareholders, and factors such as the image and personal lives of individual company members may alter the confidence of the company's share-price independent to its financial merits, account sheet and objective performance indicators. At a global level, many traders openly buy and sell stocks based on 'hunches' rather than absolute fact, and some economic decisions are also derived from personal belief systems and religious thought. As a result one can consider economics as equivalent to epidemiological psychology or behavioural trends in many ways. Here a Civilomic score may offer novel mechanistic elements in society that may be modulated to enhance international financial health, while alternatively it may identify novel economic targets to modify with the aim of achieving civilization's ideals, such as stronger and enhanced societies.

Interestingly, the current Kardashev civilization score was approximately 0.725 (based on the Sagan–Kardashev formula of $K = (\log_{10}[\text{Power-6}])/10$) in 2013 and 0.7 in 1970. Global GDP is approximately \$75 trillion, and was approximately $3.3 trillion in 1970. From such data sets, an equation describing a Kardashev civilization score through GDP can be arrived at to follow these trends and also offer forecasting insights regarding future civilization scores:

$$\text{Civilomic Score} = (\log_{10}[\text{GDP}] \times 0.0525).$$

Based on this preliminary iteration of the Civilomic score, a Kardashev civilization status of 'I' will be achieved by the world at a global GDP value of $100 quintillion (a value × 10 to the power of 18). While such a Civilomic score closely mirrors that of the Kardashev score using the simple formula of logGDP and the constant 0.0525, the pure concept of the model can go beyond that of the numerical value of the Kardashev score as its core message is one where civilization can be correlated to national wealth status indicators. Consequently whether the constant of 0.0525 is used to describe this association or whether an alternate one is utilized to achieve another score, this does not detract from the trend that national wealth status (in this case measured through GDP) may be used to model and quantify civilization.

The benefits of this method include its ability to capture and reflect on civilization's multifactorial socio-political and economic fluctuations through the measure of GDP. This technique is therefore sensitive to the inherent fluctuations demonstrated by global GDP including the many elements of global change, which vary according to geo-politics, population effects, scientific discoveries, environmental elements and global status.

However, there are some potential limitations with this approach. Some authorities consider the Kardashev scale as a thought exercise for assessing extraterrestrial civilizations. If the modified civilization scale is not applied as a global world scale, but at a country-specific level, it may lead to miscalculations due to factors of derived energetic efficiency. For example, a country that introduces measures to reduce energy use, e.g. by mandating more fuel-efficient cars, would demonstrate a lower civilization score. There is also a concept of the decoupling (potential or actual) between economic growth and energy use, where GDP may grow without energy use growing in tandem. If such decoupling does occur, it would not necessarily follow that the countries in question would become less civilized as a result. Clearly energy efficiency can be considered a strong determinant of enhanced civilization, and one hypothetical method to address the paradox of applying this scale at an individual state level would be to use it in terms of potential energy use; for example, assessing that state on how much energy it could use if it wished to, rather than how much it actually uses in a specific year. Nevertheless, the forecast for global energy use in the immediate future does not demonstrate a likelihood of decoupling. Furthermore, there are no validated tools for assessing or quantifying 'the potential ability' to generate energy so that in practical terms the described application of the Kardashev scale still offers a practical and useful message; particularly as GDP could be developed as the main estimate of global civilization which would not be affected by inaccuracies and complexities in accounting for the conceivable state-level 'energy efficiency paradox'.

The assessment of civilization through GDP also carries potential limitations that overlap with those of measuring welfare and well-being through GDP. These include (Figure 6.3):

1. Flaws in measuring GDP
2. Financial shortcomings of GDP
3. GDP paradoxes

The measurement of GDP is by definition a calculation of an aggregate value so that it does not precisely consider

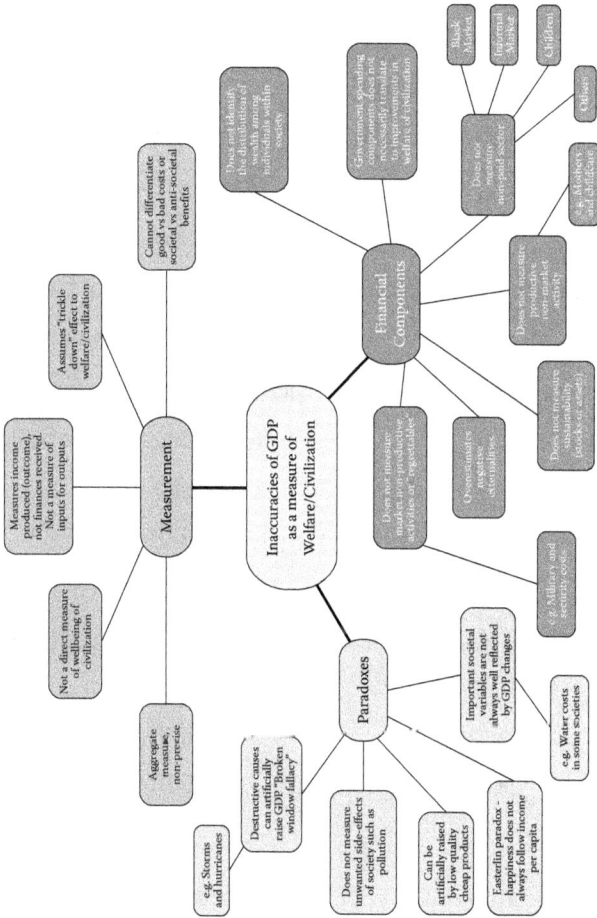

Figure 6.3 Inaccuracies of GDP as a measure of welfare and civilization.

robust characteristics or endpoints for well-being or civilization. GDP measures income produced as a primary outcome and cannot account for finances generated or received. As a result, it does not offer a direct stratification of societal outputs for inputs. In terms of welfare and society, GDP requires a fundamental supposition that can be contested by its assumption of a 'trickle-down effect' where GDP will consequentially have an effect on society. It also carries the complexity that it simply measures all costs and cannot differentiate 'good' versus 'bad' costs to society, leading to inaccuracies in calculating positive or negative dose-response effects on ensuing downstream effects on society.In terms of financial characteristics, GDP also carries several limitations. One major component of GDP calculation is governmental spending. While this is an important component of the financial sector, governmental expenditure does not necessarily translate into tangible welfare or civilization effects, but may reflect the realpolitik of each nation state so that it may only be proxy for societal good. As a financial measure, GDP fails to reflect finances in the non-paid sector, which can represent a significant portion of daily monetary exchange. Furthermore, it cannot assess productive non-market activities such as childcare. It is essentially a 'snapshot' tool, so cannot measure sustainability through stocks or assets. It tends to overestimate negative externalities and does not measure market non-productive activities such as the military and security costs. Although it does not measure the distribution of wealth, this may not be an adverse issue when measuring global civilization as an overall measure is required for calculating civilization at the global level.

There are also some paradoxes of GDP that may require attention when interpreting its value for welfare and civilization. These include Frederic Bastiat's 1850 'broken window fallacy' whereby negative societal effects such as structural and civic damage can lead to a surge in financial turnover (including repairs and replacements) to increase GDP value. Furthermore, GDP cannot account for unwanted side effects of society such as pollution, which has a strong negative impact on modern civilization. Other proxy measures of civilization such as happiness and well-being are not necessarily reflected by financial GDP trends which can be demonstrated though Easterlin's paradox in which happiness does not directly follow income per capita. In some circumstances GDP can be artificially inflated or deflated through mechanisms such as flooding a market with a large volume of very cheap products. Other societal situations that carry a heavy impact on civilization and hygiene levels (such as water supply) may already exist and therefore may not act as a source of current societal expenditure, and hence would not be reflected in the GDP of some states.

As a result of these possible inaccuracies, other measures of well-being, welfare and happiness have been developed and are continuing to be introduced. These include the Human Development Index (measuring life length, education and GDP per capita), the Genuine Progress Indicator (using GDP but adjusting for several factors including household value, volunteer work, income distribution and the costs of pollution and crime), and the Happy Planet Index (product of life satisfaction and life expectancy divided by the ecological footprint). In addition to GDP, these measures aim to capture indicators of well-being, society and ecology, although none have to date been universally acknowledged, applied, validated or disseminated. Despite the conditional shortcomings of GDP, it nevertheless offers some clear advantages for offering a perception into civilization:

1. It remains to be an acknowledged and universally accepted common yardstick that is applied consistently at the world level to assess global economic status.

2. It is rigorously calculated globally according to well-defined and well-understood parameters.

3. It is readily recognized and comprehended by a large proportion of society including the lay public.

4. In view of its almost universal awareness, individuals, states and governments act upon GDP results to enhance national and international progression.

The application of the Civilomic score to identify mankind's civilization level through global economics offers the novel perception of our current world through the generation of an objective and quantifiable score. As there is a broad range of tools to dissect and categorize global GDP, this provides a new opportunity to assess and ultimately improve mankind's level of civilization through enhanced academic scrutiny and optimized financial policies. These elements reinforce the positions of surgeons and healthcare practitioners within society and help identify the contributors that both support and drive civilization and also highlight the role of a holistic view when managing the well-being of an individual or more broadly a whole nation.

7 Approaches and Leadership

1. In war, the general receives his commands from the sovereign, collects his army and concentrates his forces.

1. The surgeon achieves decisions through best evidence (evidence-based practice), experience, ethics and patients' needs. Patient preference is important and all procedures should be performed on patients who are fully and appropriately consented regarding the benefits and risks of their operative procedure.

2. When in difficult country, do not encamp. In country where high roads intersect, join hands with your allies. Do not linger in dangerously isolated positions. In hemmed-in situations, you must resort to stratagem. In desperate position, you must fight.

2. Try to avoid areas of operative risk and vulnerable anatomy where possible. This can reduce the risk of surgical

complications. Modern intra-operative imaging such as the use of augmented reality in robotic surgery (to highlight danger areas such as nerves) or in-built constraints to prevent damage to a particular territory may aid the surgeon in bypassing anatomically susceptible areas.

3. There are roads which must not be followed, armies which must be not attacked, towns which must not be besieged, positions which must not be contested, commands of the sovereign which must not be obeyed.

3. There are surgical approaches which must not be followed, and tissues that must not be incised (for example specific nerves and vessels that following an incision may lead to unwanted haemorrhage and nerve damage). It is axiomatic that the *trauma of surgery* should not outweigh its benefits, or it would render the process of surgery illogical. Surgery should only be performed on patients when the risk–benefit ratio is favourable for the patient.

4. The general who thoroughly understands the advantages that accompany variation of tactics knows how to handle his troops.

4. The surgeon who thoroughly understands the advantages that accompany variation of surgical approaches (and

only employs these in the correct setting) can perform the correct procedure for each patient.

For example, the disease of achalasia of the oesophagus (incomplete relaxation of the lower oesophageal sphincter associated with increased tone and failure of oesophageal peristalsis) can be managed *externally* by traditional fully open or minimally invasive keyhole (laparoscopic) Heller myotomy, which cuts the muscles at the *cardia,* or lower oesophageal sphincter, or botulinum toxin (Botox) injection into these muscles. However, this condition can also be managed by *systemic therapies* such as lifestyle changes and drug therapy (calcium channel blockers, nitrates and proton pump inhibitors). It can also be treated *internally* by endoscopic pneumatic dilation or by peroral endoscopic myotomy (POEM). Similarly, biliary pancreatitis or cholelithiasis (gallstones) with biliary obstruction can be treated with endoscopic retrograde cholangiopancreatography (ERCP) and sphincterotomy with subsequent cholecystectomy (gallbladder removal), or by laparoscopic cholecystectomy and intra-operative cholangiography with possible bile duct exploration (either direct or trans-cystic). Each technique has its own risk–benefit profile and the surgeon

who appreciates these can offer the most beneficial procedure for each individual patient.

*5. The general who does not understand these, may be well
acquainted with the configuration of the country, yet he will
not be able to turn his knowledge to practical account.*

5. The surgeon who does not understand these, may be well
acquainted with the anatomy of the body, yet he will not be
able to turn his knowledge to practical account.

*6. So, the student of war who is unversed in the art of war of
varying his plans, even though he be acquainted with the Five
Advantages, will fail to make the best use of his men.*

6. So, the student of surgery who is unversed in the art
of operative strategy of varying his plans, even though
he is acquainted with the five constants, will fail to make
the best use of his staff and might not be able to perform the
best or safest operation in each circumstance.

*7. Hence in the wise leader's plans, considerations of advantage
and of disadvantage will be blended together.*

7. As a result of the consent process, considerations of
advantage and of disadvantage will be blended together.

*8. If our expectation of advantage be tempered in this way, we
may succeed in accomplishing the essential part of our schemes.*

8. If our expectation of advantage be tempered in this way, we may succeed in accomplishing the essential part of our therapeutic strategies.

9. If, on the other hand, in the midst of difficulties we are always ready to seize an advantage, we may extricate ourselves from misfortune.

9. If, on the other hand, in the midst of difficulties we are always ready to seize an advantage, we may extricate ourselves from misfortune. Consequently, we can act on some opportunities a disease displays, such as the existence of disease-specific biomarkers or immunity antigens (demonstrable with some cancers) which can be targeted for pharmacotherapy, or augmented reality to guide our operations for better margin clearance and better post-operative outcomes.

10. Reduce the hostile chiefs by inflicting damage on them; and make trouble for them, and keep them constantly engaged; hold out specious allurements, and make them rush to any given point.

10. Reduce surgical collateral damage by precision and efficient movements; never operate haphazardly or rush unnecessarily; make progress but operate in a safe manner to ensure the best surgical result.

11. The art of war teaches us to rely not on the likelihood of the enemy's not coming, but on our own readiness to receive him; not on the chance of his not attacking, but rather on the fact that we have made our position unassailable.

11. The art of surgery teaches us to rely on our own readiness to address disease – not by luck, but rather on the fact that we have made our procedure robust and unassailable.

12. There are five dangerous faults which may affect a general: (1) Recklessness, which leads to destruction; (2) cowardice, which leads to capture; (3) a hasty temper, which can be provoked by insults; (4) a delicacy of honour which is sensitive to shame; (5) over-solicitude for his men, which exposes him to worry and trouble.

12. Excluding surgical skills, there are five dangerous character faults which may affect a surgeon: (1) recklessness, which leads to destruction; (2) cowardice, which leads to disease progression; (3) a hasty temper, which can be provoked by insults; (4) arrogance, which can lead to over-confidence and surgical mistakes (diseases rarely allow for complacency); (5) dishonesty, which can lead to direct miscommunications and harm.

13. These are the five besetting sins of a general, ruinous to the conduct of war.

13. These are the five besetting sins of a surgeon, ruinous to the conduct of operations.

14. When an army is overthrown and its leader slain, the cause will surely be found among these five dangerous faults. Let them be a subject of meditation.

14. In addition to disease status and technical issues, these are five dangerous faults. Let them be a subject of meditation.

8 Anatomy

1. We may distinguish six kinds of terrain, to wit: (1) Accessible ground; (2) entangling ground; (3) temporizing ground; (4) narrow passes; (5) precipitous heights; (6) positions at a great distance from the enemy.

1. We may distinguish six kinds of anatomy, to wit: (1) bones, (2) nerves, (3) muscles, (4) vasculature, (5) lymphatic system, (6) organs. These can be studied through (a) gross or macroscopic anatomy (regional, systemic, surface); (b) microscopic anatomy (cytology for cells and histology for tissues); (c) molecular anatomy; and (d) developmental anatomy (embryology).

2. Ground which can be freely traversed by both sides is called accessible.

3. With regard to ground of this nature, be before the enemy in occupying the raised and sunny spots, and carefully guard your line of supplies. Then you will be able to fight with advantage.

4. Ground which can be abandoned but is hard to re-occupy is called entangling.

5. From a position of this sort, if the enemy is unprepared, you may sally forth and defeat him. But if the enemy is prepared for your coming, and you fail to defeat him, then, return being impossible, disaster will ensue.

6. When the position is such that neither side will gain by making the first move, it is called temporizing ground.

7. In a position of this sort, even though the enemy should offer us an attractive bait, it will be advisable not to stir forth, but rather to retreat, thus enticing the enemy in his turn; then, when part of his army has come out, we may deliver our attack with advantage.

8. With regard to narrow passes, if you can occupy them first, let them be strongly garrisoned and await the advent of the enemy.

9. Should the army forestall you in occupying a pass, do not go after him if the pass is fully garrisoned, but only if it is weakly garrisoned.

10. With regard to precipitous heights, if you are beforehand with your adversary, you should occupy the raised and sunny spots, and there wait for him to come up.

11. If the enemy has occupied them before you, do not follow him, but retreat and try to entice him away.

2–11. Be mindful that a surgeon does not operate on only one type of anatomy. An orthopaedic surgeon does not simply perform surgery on bones but performs surgery that manages the musculoskeletal system, bones and bone-associated diseases. A colorectal surgeon does not only operate on the colon and rectum but considers the blood vessels and nerves that supply the hindgut, such that each operation requires adequate surgical access (such as laparotomy or laparoscopy), haemostasis and awareness of regional and systemic body tissue in order to perform surgery on the colorectal region.

Fundamentally, surgery involves retraction, exposure and tissue planes. The knowledge and appreciation of anatomy allows the application of these principles to complete a successful operative procedure.

12. If you are situated at a great distance from the enemy, and the strength of the two armies is equal, it is not easy to provoke a battle, and fighting will be to your disadvantage.

12. Try not to operate at a distance from the disease focus. If this is necessary, however, you must plan your incision to ensure adequate visualization of your operative field. The

innovation of minimally invasive technologies such as laparoscopy, thoracoscopy and robotics has offered this possibility since the late twentieth century.

13. These six are the principles connected with Earth. The general who has attained a responsible post must be careful to study them.

13. These six anatomies correspond with the morphology of the human body. The surgeon who has attained a responsible post must be careful to study them.

14. Now an army is exposed to six several calamities, not arising from natural causes, but from faults for which the general is responsible. These are: (1) Flight; (2) insubordination; (3) collapse; (4) ruin; (5) disorganization; (6) rout.

15. Other conditions being equal, if one force is hurled against another ten times its size, the result will be the flight of the former.

14, 15. Now a surgeon is exposed to six several calamities (pathologies), not arising from mysterious causes but from a combination of inheritance and environmental factors. These are (1) cancer; (2) ischaemia (lack of blood supply); (3) trauma; (4) structure and tissue insufficiency;

(5) infection and inflammation; and (6) nutrition and metabolic dysfunction.

16. When the common soldiers are too strong and their officers too weak, the result is insubordination. When the officers are too strong and the common soldiers too weak, the result is collapse.

17. When the higher officers are angry and insubordinate, and on meeting the enemy give battle on their own account from a feeling of resentment, before the commander-in-chief can tell whether or no he is in a position to fight, the result is ruin.

16, 17. For operative success, there must be a harmonious team working and a successful dialogue between all staff involved in an operation (including surgeons, anaesthetists, nurses and operative theatre practitioners among many others). The surgeon should confidently guide each step of the procedure and support his team with humanity and awareness of their individual abilities and strengths. This harmony enhances the likelihood of successful surgical outcomes.

18. When the general is weak and without authority; when his orders are not clear and distinct; when there are no fixed duties assigned to officers and men, and the ranks are formed in a slovenly haphazard manner, the result is utter disorganization.

18. When the surgeon is weak and without authority, when plans and requests are not clear and distinct, when there are no fixed duties assigned to his or her surgical team, and the operative staff are formed in a slovenly haphazard manner, the result is utter disorganization.

19. When a general, unable to estimate the enemy's strength, allows an inferior force to engage a larger one, or hurls a weak detachment against a powerful one, and neglects to place picked soldiers in the front rank, the result must be rout.

19. If a surgeon fails to perform adequate pre-operative preparation or investigations and is not knowledgeable of the patient's disease process or stage and grade before surgery, then surgical outcomes will likely be poor.

20. These are six ways of courting defeat, which must be carefully noted by the general who has attained a responsible post.

20. These are several ways of courting defeat, which must be carefully noted by the surgeon who has attained a responsible post.

21. The natural formation of the country is the soldier's best ally; but a power of estimating the adversary, of controlling the forces of victory, and of shrewdly calculating difficulties, dangers and distances, constitutes the test of a great general.

21. Knowledge of anatomy and tissue planes is the surgeon's best ally; but a power of estimating disease stage and grade, of controlling physiology, and of shrewdly calculating difficulties, dangers and operative strategy, constitutes the test of a great surgeon.

22. He who knows these things, and in fighting puts his knowledge into practice, will win his battles. He who knows them not, nor practices them, will surely be defeated.

22. He who knows these things, and in surgery puts his knowledge into practice, will succeed in his or her operations. He who knows them not, nor practises them, will surely be unsuccessful.

23. If fighting is sure to result in victory, then you must fight, even though the ruler forbid it; if fighting will not result in victory, then you must not fight even at the ruler's bidding.

23. The key is to offer the best surgical outcome with consideration of the patient who has been adequately consented for the procedures that he or she will undergo.

24. The general who advances without coveting fame and retreats without fearing disgrace, whose only thought is to protect his country and do good service for his sovereign, is the jewel of the kingdom.

24. The surgeon who advances without coveting fame and retreats without fearing disgrace, whose only thought is to combat disease and do good service for his patient, is the jewel of the healthcare system.

9 The Nine Elements of the Surgical Sieve and Surgical Specialities

1. The art of war recognizes nine varieties of ground: (1) Dispersive ground; (2) facile ground; (3) contentious ground; (4) open ground; (5) ground of intersecting highways; (6) serious ground; (7) difficult ground; (8) hemmed-in ground; (9) desperate ground.

1. The art of surgery recognizes nine varieties of disease aetiology: (1) surroundings and environmental issues of patients; (2) unknown and idiopathic conditions; (3) neoplasia and cancer; (4) diseases of toxins, metabolites and pharmacological drugs; (5) sepsis, infections and dysfunctions of immunity (it is important to remember zoonosis or infectious disease transmitted between species – these have sometimes been overlooked; (6) vascular and haematological diseases; (7) disorders as a result from trauma and

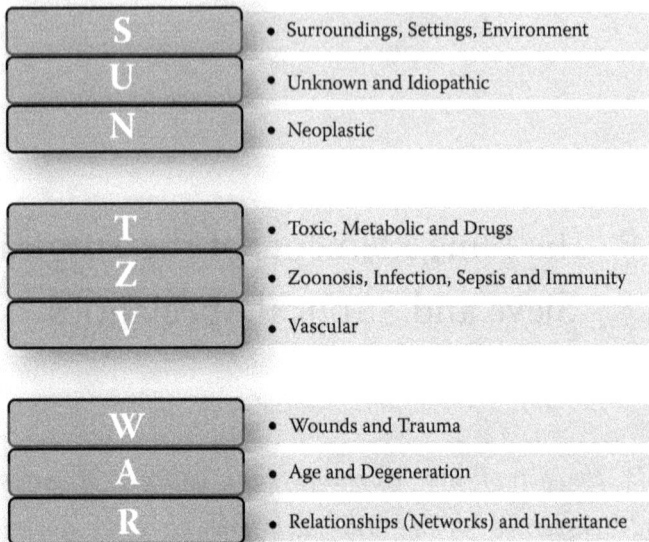

Figure 9.1 Surgical sieve.

wounds; (8) diseases of age and degeneration; and (9) diseases of associations, relationships and networks of society (including those of obesity and drug addiction). These can be summarized by a 'surgical sieve' in the form of the author's mnemonic for assessing patients: SUN TZV WAR (Figure 9.1).

One core paradigm is to not confuse symptoms with the underlying pathology; diseases can cause symptoms though the resolution of symptoms does not always equate that the underlying disease is also resolved. Doctors are still characterized by their individual and traditional specialties when managing patients. Surgical specialties include otolaryngology (ear, nose and throat surgery), cardiothoracic, vascular (cardiovascular), breast, urology, plastics and reconstructive (including cosmetic), coloproctology (colorectal or lower gastrointestinal), hepatobiliary, upper gastrointestinal (for both cancerous and benign disease and including bariatric or metabolic surgery), paediatric, orthopaedics and trauma, neurosurgery, maxillofacial, ophthalmology and obstetrics and gynaecological surgery. These traditional boundaries are changeable and surgeons are sometimes characterized according to system specialities, such as pelvic floor or peripheral limb specialists.

10 Firesticks and Haemostasis

1. There are five ways of attacking with fire. The first is to burn soldiers in their camp; the second is to burn stores; the third is to burn baggage trains; the fourth is to burn arsenals and magazines; the fifth is to hurl dropping fire amongst the enemy.

1. There are five ways of achieving haemostasis of bleeding vasculature: (i) Electrocoagulation (diathermy and coblation) through monopolar diathermy (traditionally known as 'firestick' or 'Bovie', named for its inventor William T. Bovie) is practised. The firestick or Bovie is an electrosurgery device that permits cutting, coagulation, cauterization, desiccation or fulguration by applying a high-frequency current through a metallic probe to a tissue. In monopolar diathermy, electrical current passes from the probe to a fixed indifferent electrode placed elsewhere on the body (typically the legs or buttocks).

(ii) Electrocoagulation through bipolar diathermy is a technique in which both electrodes are on the same instrument (such as forceps), and the area for electrocoagulation is placed between the two probe surfaces so that current passes between the probes and not through the patient. This offers focussed electrocoagulation that can be applied in precision settings such as microsurgery, or in situations when through-body current is unadvisable such as in the presence of a pacemaker. Examples include Kleppinger bipolar forceps and LigaSure™ technology (Valleylab, Boulder, Colorado), which offers a bipolar diathermy platform with advanced electrical algorithms and tissue-sensing feedback.

(iii) Ultrasonic devices that apply high-frequency ultrasound achieve electrocoagulation through mechanical energetic breakdown of protein to create a local coagulum. An example is the Harmonic scalpel (Ethicon, Inc., Somerville, New Jersey).

(iv) Laser-based systems, typically used in ophthalmology, obstetrics and gynaecology, and dentistry are also used. An example in ophthalmology is the LASIK (laser-assisted in situ keratomileusis) procedure. Several types of lasers can be used for electrosurgery, including diode lasers and Nd:YAG (neodymium-doped yttrium aluminium garnet; $Nd:Y_3Al_5O_{12}$) lasers.

(v) Magnetic electrosurgery such as the ferromagnetic dissection device, FMwand (Domain Surgical, Inc. Salt Lake City, Utah), which offers an inductive magnetic field effect on a sealing tool with no magnetic-induced effect in the tissue. Vascular sealing takes place through inductive rapid heating and subsequent cool-down.

2. In order to carry out an attack, we must have means available. The material for raising fire should always be kept in readiness.

2. In order to perform an operation, we must have means available. Haemostatic devices should always be kept in readiness.

3. There is a proper season for making attacks with fire, and special days for starting a conflagration.

3. There is a proper time for applying haemostatic devices; use them judiciously, as they carry side effects including tissue damage. Excessive use can also damage the surgeon and theatre staff. The smoke from diathermy has been analysed to reveal traces of diseased tissue, microbes and infectious agents.

4. The proper season is when the weather is very dry; the special days are those when the moon is in the constellations of the

Sieve, the Wall, the Wing or the Cross-bar; for these four are all days of rising wind.

4. The proper use of a haemostatic device should be when faced with a known target for tissue cutting or sealing.

5. In attacking with fire, one should be prepared to meet five possible developments:

5. Haemostatic devices offer five possible effects, which follow.

6. (1) When fire breaks out inside to enemy's camp, respond at once with an attack from without.

6. (i) Coagulation (forming blood clots by thrombogenesis)

7. (2) If there is an outbreak of fire, but the enemy's soldiers remain quiet, bide your time and do not attack.

7. (ii) Cutting and dissection

8. (3) When the force of the flames has reached its height, follow it up with an attack, if that is practicable; if not, stay where you are.

8. (iii) Cauterization (localized burning) and dessication (extreme dryness)

9. (4) If it is possible to make an assault with fire from without, do not wait for it to break out within, but deliver your attack at a favorable moment.

9. (iv) Fulguration (tissue destruction)

10. (5) When you start a fire, be to windward of it. Do not attack from the leeward.

10. (v) Anastomoses through tissue fusion

11. A wind that rises in the daytime lasts long, but a night breeze soon falls.

11. In an ideal environment, the application of haemostatic device should be in the absence of a local suffusion of bio-fluids such as blood.

12. In every army, the five developments connected with fire must be known, the movements of the stars calculated, and a watch kept for the proper days.

12. In every surgical team, the haemostatic devices should be readily connected and prepared in anticipation of each operative procedure. Staff should be familiar with the devices available and how to use them.

13. Hence those who use fire as an aid to the attack show intelligence; those who use water as an aid to the attack gain an accession of strength.

13. Hence those who apply haemostatic agents show intelligence.

14. By means of water, an enemy may be intercepted, but not robbed of all his belongings.

14. Saline (adequately warmed for body temperatures) or surgical gauze can be applied to wash away excessive bio-fluids such as blood in order to identify bleeding sources for electrocoagulation.

15. Unhappy is the fate of one who tries to win his battles and succeed in his attacks without cultivating the spirit of enterprise; for the result is waste of time and general stagnation.

15. Unhappy is the fate of one who tries to operate and succeed against the disease process without cultivating the spirit of enterprise; for the result is waste of time and general stagnation.

16. Hence the saying: The enlightened ruler lays his plans well ahead; the good general cultivates his resources.

16. Hence the enlightened healthcare institution plans well ahead; the good surgeon cultivates his or her resources.

17. Move not unless you see an advantage; use not your troops unless there is something to be gained; fight not unless the position is critical.

17. Do not incise or cut tissues unless you see an advantage; use not your surgical tools unless there is something to be gained; operate not unless the procedure is necessary.

18. No ruler should put troops into the field merely to gratify his own spleen; no general should fight a battle simply out of pique.

18. No patient should request surgery 'to gratify his own spleen' (for example as in Munchausen or hospital addiction syndrome); no surgeon should operate simply out of pique.

19. If it is to your advantage, make a forward move; if not, stay where you are.

19. If it is to the surgeon's and patient's advantage, perform surgery or make operative progress; if not, do not operate unnecessarily.

20. Anger may in time change to gladness; vexation may be succeeded by content.

20. Anger may change to gladness, vexation may be succeeded by content because unnecessary procedures will not be undertaken and so operative risks will be avoided, and ultimately patients will not be harmed by surgery – *Primum non nocere*. Where necessary surgery can be performed in the event that risk–benefit ratios allow for this, and the patient can receive the highest quality care and enjoy the advantages of enhanced outcomes and well-being.

21. But a kingdom that has once been destroyed can never come again into being; nor can the dead ever be brought back to life.

21. But a body or organ that has once been destroyed can never come again into being; nor can the dead ever be brought back to life.

22. Hence the enlightened ruler is heedful, and the good general full of caution. This is the way to keep a country at peace and an army intact.

22. Hence the enlightened healthcare institution is heedful, and the good surgeon full of caution. This is the way to keep a population healthy and a health system intact.

11 Imaging

1. Raising a host of a hundred thousand men and marching them great distances entails heavy loss on the people and a drain on the resources of the State. The daily expenditure will amount to a thousand ounces of silver. There will be commotion at home and abroad, and men will drop down exhausted on the highways. As many as seven hundred thousand families will be impeded in their labour.

1. Preparing a patient for an operation, performing the procedure, and finally caring for the recovering patient all consume the resources of the surgeon, the hospital, the healthcare system and the patients.

2. Hostile armies may face each other for years, striving for the victory which is decided in a single day. This being so, to remain in ignorance of the enemy's condition simply because one grudges the outlay of a hundred ounces of silver in honours and emoluments, is the height of inhumanity.

2. Fighting a disease process may take many years to combat, but victory against disease may be decided by a surgery on a single day. This being so, to remain in ignorance of the disease's status simply because one begrudges the effort of preparing for a procedure, is the height of inhumanity.

3. One who acts thus is no leader of men, no present help to his sovereign, no master of victory.

3. One who acts thus is no surgeon, no present help to his patient, no master of victory.

4. Thus, what enables the wise sovereign and the good general to strike and conquer, and achieve things beyond the reach of ordinary men, is foreknowledge.

4. Thus, what enables the wise patient and the good surgeon to strike and conquer disease is diagnostic foreknowledge.

5. Now this foreknowledge cannot be elicited from spirits; it cannot be obtained inductively from experience, nor by any deductive calculation.

5. Now this diagnostic foreknowledge cannot be guessed. While traditional clinical history signs and examination may offer some anatomico-pathological diagnostic accuracy,

often higher-precision accuracy is needed to identify disease location and extent. Disease processes may be hidden by overlying body organs or may be too small or the wrong scale for visualization by human senses. Accurate diagnoses may therefore be achieved through imaging modalities.

6. Knowledge of the enemy's dispositions can only be obtained from other men.

6. Accurate knowledge of the patient's disease location and status can be obtained with imaging technology. Invasive imaging by definition carries risks of a surgical intervention such as trauma and bleeding, but non-invasive imaging can avoid the risks of invasive diagnostic procedures.

7. Hence the use of spies, of whom there are five classes: (1) Local spies; (2) inward spies; (3) converted spies; (4) doomed spies; (5) surviving spies.

7. Hence in addition to standard invasive surgical methods of diagnostic imaging (such as open surgery, laparoscopy and endoscopy) which can offer tissues for analysis (such as histology), there are five classes of non-invasive methodologies: (1) X-ray (X-radiation, or Röntgen radiation) and radionuclide-based (radioactive isotopes or radioisotopes). Examples of X-ray–based modalities include standard

radiographs, computed tomography, X-ray angiography and fluoroscopy. Radionuclide-based diagnostic tests are used in nuclear medicine scans such as thallium scans and technetium scans. (2) Magnetic scans such as magnetic resonance imaging (MRI) also known as nuclear magnetic resonance imaging (NMRI), or magnetic resonance tomography (MRT). These define topographical anatomy and disease location. Nuclear magnetic resonance (NMR) spectroscopy can offer high-precision biochemical spectrographic profiles of biofluids and tissues. (3) Ionizing modalities such as mass spectrometry (MS) can also offer high-precision biochemical and isoptopic data regarding biofluids and tissues. (4) Sonographic-based modalities such as ultrasound, echocardiography and duplex (which offers real-time flow imaging by adding Doppler flow to conventional ultrasonography). (5) Infrared modalities such as near-infrared spectroscopy (NIRS) and pulse oximetry.

8. When these five kinds of spy are all at work, none can discover the secret system. This is called "divine manipulation of the threads." It is the sovereign's most precious faculty.

8. When these five kinds of non-invasive imaging are all at work, a great deal of pathological information can be discerned to arm the surgeon with pre-operative knowledge.

The surgeon can then prepare for the operation so as to ensure maximum safety and patient outcome. Sun Tzu called this the 'divine manipulation of the threads'. 'Pre-operative diagnostic evaluation' is the patient's and surgeon's most precious faculty.

9. Having LOCAL SPIES means employing the services of the inhabitants of a district.

9. X-ray modalities including computed tomography (CT) scans are very good at diagnosing disease according to distinct anatomical landmarks; for example, bone fractures and cancer presence can be accurately assessed. Techniques such as positron emission tomography (PET) are able to exploit the characteristics of disease, such as the increased metabolic activity of malignant tissue, in order to localize a tumour and its spread, providing vital diagnostic information when planning surgery.

10. Having INWARD SPIES, making use of officials of the enemy.

10. Magnetic modalities such as MRI offer excellent soft tissue contrast so they are very good at assessing disease in ligaments, tendons, the brain and the spinal cord. They have the drawback of contraindication for metallic

fragments, prosthesis clips or devices (such as pacemakers) and are usually more expensive than X-ray modalities.

11. Having CONVERTED SPIES, getting hold of the enemy's spies and using them for our own purposes.

11. It is sometimes the disease processes that hijack out sensing systems and use them against the human body in a pathological setting. For example, hypoxia-inducible factors (HIFs) sense tissue oxygenation levels so that a decrease in oxygenation via hypoxia results in HIFs acting as transcription factors to regulate increased blood supply through local vessel generation (angiogenesis), energy delivery (glycolysis) and the enhancement of oxygen carrying ability (through erythropoietin). However, these important sensing systems can also be used against health as they can be hijacked by cancers to enhance tumour growth, metastasis and create an environment that favours tumour generation.

12. Having DOOMED SPIES, doing certain things openly for purposes of deception, and allowing our spies to know of them and report them to the enemy.

12. Conversely, we can use the sensing systems that have been hijacked by cancer as our targets to attack cancerous disease. As such we can use natural molecular sensing

agents as 'double agents' through which we can combat disease. For example, several pharmacological anti-cancer agents have been designed to target the HIF-1 pathway.

13. SURVIVING SPIES, finally, are those who bring back news from the enemy's camp.

13. Furthermore, we can also 'bootstrap' onto the biological communications of disease processes to target them. For example, many cancer processes rely on lymph node involvement and spread, but as surgeons we can take advantage of such systems to identify disease sources and tracks with which to excise or treat pathology. This can be demonstrated in sentinel lymph node biopsy, where surgeons can stain the diseased lymph tracks so that they can target lymph nodes that first drain a primary tumour site. By doing so they can excise these nodes to stage and minimize any further elements of cancer spread (metastases and micrometastases), and thereby improve cancer outcomes. Staining techniques for sentinel lymph nodes include radiological staining with radioactive isotopes (to be assessed by radioactivity gamma-detecting instruments), lymphoscintigraphy (with or without radiological support), dyes that can be assessed by visual inspection or fluorescence, or a combination of these methods.

14. Hence it is that which none in the whole army are more intimate relations to be maintained than with spies. None should be more liberally rewarded. In no other business should greater secrecy be preserved.

14. Hence it is that which none in the whole surgical unit are more intimate relations to be maintained than diagnosticians and diagnostic imaging experts (such as radiologists). They should be liberally praised and respected as colleagues who work as collaborators. Their role in surgical multidisciplinary meetings and operative strategy is key as they can clarify and reveal the exact location, spread and involvement of disease to enhance surgical outcomes.

15. Spies cannot be usefully employed without a certain intuitive sagacity.

15. Imaging cannot be usefully employed without a certain intuitive sagacity. You must have a diagnostic question in mind, or you are looking blindly and your diagnostic yield will be poor.

16. They cannot be properly managed without benevolence and straightforwardness.

16. You cannot interact with radiological colleagues without benevolence and straightforwardness.

17. Without subtle ingenuity of mind, one cannot make certain of the truth of their reports.

17. Without subtle ingenuity of mind and awareness of the underlying disease process, one cannot make certain of the interpretation of their (radiological) reports.

18. Be subtle! be subtle! and use your spies for every kind of business.

18. Be inquisitive! and use non-invasive imaging wherever appropriate.

19. If a secret piece of news is divulged by a spy before the time is ripe, he must be put to death together with the man to whom the secret was told.

19. Unnecessary testing or imaging done without a question is akin to screening blindly for a disease and will not offer optimum diagnostic yield.

20. Whether the object be to crush an army, to storm a city, or to assassinate an individual, it is always necessary to begin by finding out the names of the attendants, the aides-de-camp, and door-keepers and sentries of the general in command. Our spies must be commissioned to ascertain these.

20. Whether the object be to operate on a disease or to target for radiotherapy or purely for diagnosis, it is always necessary to interpret imaging from established anatomical landmarks and compare current scans to previous ones where available to assess changes according to time. Multiple imaging modalities can be used concurrently, as the overlapping information may offer an increased sensitivity, specificity and diagnostic accuracy. For example, concurrent ultrasound, mammography and clinical assessment of breast examination (triple assessment) ensures a high diagnostic yield in testing for breast cancer.

21. The enemy's spies who have come to spy on us must be sought out, tempted with bribes, led away and comfortably housed. Thus they will become converted spies and available for our service.

21. While disease processes are not 'sentient' or 'conscious', they do have the ability to react to medical manipulation. For example, microorganisms can develop resistance to antibiotic therapy, so the judicious use of intervention and therapy is necessary to prevent disease resistance and recurrence.

22. It is through the information brought by the converted spy that we are able to acquire and employ local and inward spies.

22. It is through the information brought by diagnostic technologies that we are able to acquire pre-emptive pathological information and prepare surgical strategy.

23. It is owing to his information, again, that we can cause the doomed spy to carry false tidings to the enemy.

23. It is owing to diagnostic information, again, that we can target diseases for surgery and intervention.

24. Lastly, it is by his information that the surviving spy can be used on appointed occasions.

24. Lastly, it is by diagnostic information that patient survival can be enhanced.

25. The end and aim of spying in all its five varieties is knowledge of the enemy; and this knowledge can only be derived, in the first instance, from the converted spy. Hence it is essential that the converted spy be treated with the utmost liberality.

25. The end and aim of non-invasive imaging in all its five varieties is knowledge of the disease; and this knowledge can only be derived, in the first instance, from appropriate technology. Hence it is essential that innovation in all things diagnostic should be considered to improve the future of surgical outcomes.

26. Of old, the rise of the Yin dynasty was due to I Chih who had served under the Hsia. Likewise, the rise of the Chou dynasty was due to Lu Ya who had served under the Yin.

26. Of old, the rise of CT scans was due to its first applicable and commercial introduction by Sir Godfrey Hounsfield (1919–2004) who was awarded the 1979 Nobel Prize for physiology or medicine. Likewise, the rise of MRI was due to its practical clinical introduction by Raymond Damadian, Paul Lauterbur and Sir Peter Mansfield. The latter two were awarded the 2003 Nobel Prize for physiology or medicine (Damadian – controversially – was excluded).

27. Hence it is only the enlightened ruler and the wise general who will use the highest intelligence of the army for purposes of spying and thereby they achieve great results. Spies are a most important element in water, because on them depends an army's ability to move.

27. Hence it is only the enlightened healthcare institution and the wise surgeon who will use the most appropriate imaging offered by diagnostic technology and clinical acumen to achieve great results. Clinical skills and diagnostic interpretation are a most important element in healthcare, because on them depends the surgeon's ability to operate.

Index

For Product Safety Concerns and Information please contact our EU
representative GPSR@taylorandfrancis.com
Taylor & Francis Verlag GmbH, Kaufingerstraße 24, 80331 München, Germany